FIRST AID

From the
Appliance Doctor,

Joseph Gagnon

Edited by Kathy Stief
Cover and Interior Photos
by Charles H. Cloud III

MASTER HANDYMAN PRESS, INC.

FIRST AID

From the Appliance Doctor,

Joseph Gagnon

Edited by Kathy Stief

Published by:

Master Handyman Press, Inc.
Post Office Box 1498
Royal Oak, MI 48068-1498 U.S.A.

First Printing 1994

Printed in the United States of America

Library of Congress Cataloging in Publication Data.
Gagnon, Joseph
    Major appliance selection,
    maintenance and repair
    Bibliography: g.

ISBN: 1-880615-50-9

*This book is dedicated to two people
who have been with me since early days.
First, my "little brother, Larry.*

*Second, to the memory of Jack Plating
of the Amana Corporation. A great friend,
teacher and one heck of an appliance man.*

Acknowledgments

I have always wanted to write a book but I never took the time until one man got me to stop procrastinating and start doing. He's the same man who is most responsible for my name being recognized on radio, America's Master Handyman and WXYT's gift to the air waves, Glenn Haege.

Esther Shapiro, the Director of Detroit's Department of Consumer Affairs, is a beautiful lady who has inspired my boldness in helping the public, made me a consultant to her office. She convinced me to produce what became her office's two most popular booklets on major appliances and gave me the confidence that maybe I could write.

I also should thank a thousand others, including:

Ted Heusel of WAAM Radio, Ann Arbor, who introduced the "Talk" concept to AM radio over forty years ago and made me comfortable in front of a microphone.

Jack Bailey of WCAR Radio, who signed me to do a weekly talk show because he trusted in my common sense and believed that I was sincere in helping consumers.

Bob Allison of WEXL, a 30 year talk veteran and a pioneer of consumer talk radio, who kept telling listeners to call me, on and off the air.

Bob Taylor of WJR, who kept sharing his microphone with me because he believed I had a message his listeners needed to hear.

Joe Madison, who first had me on the air on WXYT, then kept the faith when he moved to WRC in Washington, DC; and now has given me an opportunity on the TPT Radio Broadcasting Network.

Michael Daisy of the *Northwest Detroiter*, who lets me help his readers with a monthly consumer column.

Kathy Stief, my editor, who prodded my words and ramblings into this manuscript.

Val, my helpmate, who made this book her own crusade, and my kids, Jennie, Megan, Shawn, Mark and Andrew, whose hang tough love gives me the strength to carry on, and gives my life its meaning.

My thanks all.

Joe Gagnon
Garden City, Michigan

Table of Contents

Introduction

This is the book I promised you.

What you are about to read is more than just a lesson on how to keep your appliances running in tip top condition. It is a brief education on the entire industry.

Knowledge is power. This book is written to make you a more powerful consumer, by a man who has spent almost thirty years in the business.

It is designed to save you cash. The first five chapters give you the information you need to be a smart "street wise" shopper. The rest of the book is on appliance selection, maintenance and repair. Follow the advice and you will save a lot of money.

At the outset, I would like to thank the editors and publishers of *Appliance Industry* magazine for permission to use statistics compiled and reported by them. Sales Volume and Market Share statistics cited in this book are from the February and March 1993 issues of that magazine.

By the end of the book you will be a better prepared consumer than 99% of your fellow customers. You will also know more about the entire industry than at least 50% of the people in the business.

As you read, grab the newspaper, or telephone book, check out what I say. There is always the chance that in your particular community the general rule is wrong. Besides, you should never believe anything just because your read it in a newspaper, book or magazine, or because you saw or heard it on TV or radio. Always make your own conclusions.

One final word, don't let this book frighten you. There are some pretty bad apples in the Appliance Industry, but there are a lot more very good ones. As always, warning about the few takes attention from the many.

The good people in the business will read this book and cheer. They are constantly looking for ways to improve their industry and improve their service to you.

The bad people will hate this book because I show you how to outwit them at their own game.

Read, enjoy, learn and save a lot of money.

Joe Gagnon,

The Appliance Doctor®

Foreword

From the point of view of a consumer educator, Joe Gagnon is a rare specimen. He is an entrepreneur and a repair specialist who teaches the public how to make their products last longer, and how to do their own repairs. In other words, he gives away what others would be selling. This book is an example.

I first met Joe at a consumer conference, several years ago. Other members of his profession would have been attending a sales meeting instead. It was immediately evident that he had a crusader's personality. Like those knights of history, Joe felt that he had a mission to drive out evil. Nothing angered him more than the antics of those who took advantage of the rest of us. He wanted to be a protector and an educator.

Joe has filled that role in Detroit's Consumer Affairs Department. As an unpaid volunteer he has investigated complaints about inferior appliance repair, and provided us with the expert information needed to determine whether or not a consumer had been cheated. He has gone to court as an expert witness when a lawsuit against a company became necessary. He has written "how-to" pamphlets on refrigerator and dryer repair, which my office distributes by the hundreds. His TV and radio programs provide the information everyone needs to gain the maximum from the money we spend on our appliances.

If I were to single out only one of Joe's contributions, it would be his successful campaign that led to the passage of a significant Michigan protective law. Joe realized that plastic dryer vent pipes were a hazard that had led to many house fires. Thanks to his persistence, any new installations must now be of metal. His educational program has led to the replacement of hundreds of old vent pipes...mine included.

By all means take advantage of this book. It may cut into Joe's business revenue, but it will help to save yours.

Esther Shapiro

Director,

City of Detroit

Consumer Affairs Department

WARNING - DISCLAIMER

This book is designed to provide general information for the appliance purchaser and user. It is sold with the understanding that the publisher and author are not engaged in rendering legal, or other professional or consultative services. If expert assistance is required, the services of competent professionals should be sought.

Every effort has been made to make this text as complete and accurate as possible, and to assure proper credit is given to various contributors, etc. However, there may be mistakes, both typographical and in content. Therefore, this text should be used only as a general guide and not as the ultimate source of information. Furthermore, this book contains information only up to the printing date.

The purpose of this book is to educate and entertain. There is no desire on the part of the author or Master Handyman Press to malign, denigrate, or disparage any person or group of people, any product or group of products, any corporation or group of corporations, any trade, profession or trade or professional association. The author and Master Handyman Press, Inc. shall have neither liability nor responsibility to any person or entity with respect to any loss or damage caused directly or indirectly by the information contained by this book.

WARNING - DISCLAIMER

Chapter 1

APPLIANCE MANUFACTURERS

Whose product is best?

More people ask me this question than any other on my radio
and TV shows and public appearances. Usually they don't just
come out and ask, people sort of slide up to me and whisper the
question out of the side of their mouth. "Joe I'm buying a
_____ (refrigerator, range, washing machine, fill in the
blanks). Which is the best?"

There is a very simple answer to this very confusing question.
You get what you pay for. There is no one magic manufacturer
who is all good, making all other manufacturers not so good. Many
manufacturers make some high quality models and some stripped
down, cheaply constructed versions designed to capture the buyer
who is strictly price shopping.

To them, it is a sophisticated marketing technique. To me, it is
very close to suicide. Let me emphasize that this technique is
perfectly legal. The manufacturers are just capitalizing on the
public's gullibility and greed, its desire and belief that it can get
something almost for nothing.

Let me tell you folks, there is no free lunch. Cheap appliances are usually the most expensive things you can buy. Up front cost may be low, but this sucker advantage is more than made up for in repeated service calls, inefficient energy use and short appliance life. The less you pay for an appliance, the less you can expect from it.

Millions of Americans can relate to the last paragraph because they have lived through the experience. Historically, appliances were all very soundly made products. America was famous for quality manufacturing and we grew up expecting a household appliance to have a service life of fifteen to twenty years.

Today many shoppers are finding that their new appliances are only lasting an average of five to seven years. My one word explanation for this short service life is that they bought "Junk."

Why did this happen? Did a gang of criminals take over the appliance industry, or what?

Now, I am not an economist, a Ph.D. college professor, or an MBA. I didn't even graduate from college. But I do have thirty years of experience in the appliance industry serving the public. Here's what I think happened.

During the Great Depression and the Second World War (I realize to most of you this is history so ancient it is almost myth. But believe it or not, it really did happen and in many ways has a direct effect on what is happening to you right now) very few appliances were sold to the American consumer. First there was no money, then the appliance industry had to turn its considerable talents to making the machine guns, hand grenades, bomb sights, etc., necessary to free the enslaved countries from fascism and make the world safe for democracy.

I'm not bragging about something grand that I did, I was only four years old when the war ended. I know that in today's world all this may sound very saccharine. But it's what actually happened folks. It's what our mums and dads and grandparents accomplished. We Canadians and Americans can take a lot of pride in what our two countries and our older generation did.

At any rate, there was this tremendous pent up demand created from years of doing without. Suddenly, the war was over. A lot of people had money in the bank and just about everybody wanted one or two of everything.

Families bought "new" electric stoves. They converted from ice boxes to refrigerators. Freezers were an awe inspiring dream. Automatic washers were enough to make most women feel faint. And dryers, oh my gosh! Clothes dryers. You mean clothing doesn't have to be hung outdoors to dry? Then we had the newest of the new. Dishwashers? Microwave ovens?

Americans went on a buying binge that lasted thirty-five or forty years. Competition was fierce. Innovation and quality drove market penetration. The average appliance lasted fifteen or twenty years.

One day the market went "OOPS". It didn't really happen over night. Growth rates slowed for a number of years. As the market became saturated, the appliance industry became what is known as a "mature" industry. Sales got harder as the emphasis changed from new to replacement units.

A company that had been making a hundred thousand units a year, might suddenly only have a replacement market of forty or fifty thousand units, and a break even point of seventy or eighty thousand units.

The head of that company would have to do everything possible to sell the additional thirty or forty thousand units necessary to keep the company from losing money. He or she would be under extreme pressure, not only to keep his or her own job, but to keep the employees jobs; from stock holders and banks to keep their profits; and from the cities and villages in which the factory was located, to keep the payrolls which had become the life blood of the communities.

I can remember back when I was responsible for the service department of a major appliance manufacturer. The service end of the business was considered a necessary evil. It often actually cost the company money. But it didn't really matter because the difference was more than made up for in escalating sales.

As the industry matured this policy ate up the already declining manufacturing profits in many companies. It is a law of business as well as nature that only the strong survive. During this period, many good companies were gobbled up by stronger competitors.

Today, although there are more than twenty-seven major appliance brands on the American Market, ownership of the entire industry is controlled by just five companies. I have a chart telling you who owns what in an Appendix at the end of the book.

Another result of this policy was that the management of many of the remaining companies had to find new ways to inject profit into their companies. One technique was changing the parts and service departments from a "necessary evil" into a profit center.

When a manufacturer turns to parts replacement as a major profit source, there is little or no incentive to improve product quality or longevity. In fact, if you are bottom line oriented, and business management has to be, it would seem the temptation would be to go the other way.

I can not say that this is the reason for the apparent lowering of quality in many companies' products. But anyone in the appliance repair industry could tell you that many manufacturers continue to use components that have a high failure rate year after year. The parts are almost never improved and the parts and service departments just keep getting busier.

This might seem short term smart, but it is long term stupid. Appliance industry CEOs should ask their opposite numbers in the Auto Industry how long it takes the public to come back after they have been lost because of poor quality.

American consumers do not enjoy being ripped off. All this will do in the final analysis is destroy brand loyalty and create irate consumers.

I can assure you that the European manufacturers are not turning a blind eye to what is happening. They are gearing up to take advantage of this opportunity. Only time will tell if our appliance industry comes to its senses before it is too late.

Enough about ancient history and philosophy. It is enough to know that right now, you the consumer have a problem when you shop for a new appliance.

There is nothing I would like more than to detail which brands we in the service industry believe have the biggest problems. If I did that, I would probably spend the rest of my life in court and could never begin to pay my legal bills.

I can't do that, but I can give you some preemptive First Aid: ways to keep from getting burned by a chaotic appliance industry. This book is filled with tips.

How to decide what to buy.

1. Don't base your buying decision on past experience with a twenty year old appliance. Many of the top brands have been completely redesigned in the past few years and are no longer made with the quality you remember.

2. Read consumer magazines and get a handle on what features you are looking for in your new appliance.

3. Before you buy, stop by two or three independent service contractors. Ask them which brands they service the least. Write down those names for further investigation.

4. Buy, beg or borrow a copy of the most recent *Consumer's Report* that reviews the type of appliance you wish to purchase. I do not agree with everything they write about appliances, but I do think *Consumer's Report* is the best single reference the smart customer has today.

   Read the articles thoroughly. Pay special attention to manufacturers that have already been recommended to you by the service industry.

5. Ask your friends and family about the appliances they have purchased and used within the past few years. Try to find one or two people who actually own the model you are zeroing in on. Compare their answers to the recommendations by *Consumers Reports* and the service industry.

6. When you have completed all of this research you are ready to confront the salesmen at your local appliance store. Ask good comprehensive questions. I list a few starters at the beginning of every appliance chapter. You'll have more of your own.

7. If you think the salesman is filling you with a lot of guff, call the manufacturer direct. The people they have handling the phones are usually very polite and very well informed. They will answer you honestly to the limit of their knowledge. If they don't know the answer, ask for the name of somebody who does.

To give you a head start on this part of the project, I have included most manufacturers toll free telephone numbers in an Appendix at the back of the book.

Please read the chapter on advertising and the chapter directly concerned with the appliance you need **before you go shopping!**

Best of luck and good hunting.

Chapter 2

APPLIANCE STORES

The first "modern" appliances I ever saw were gasoline powered washing machines. They were quite often sold off the back end of the retailer's pickup truck. More often than not he demonstrated the product in the customer's home.

I have often thought that he must have been a very happy man. He was showing the consumer a new invention that would free women from a life of constant drudgery and revolutionize the American home. In most cases, he not only made the sale, he made both a good, honest profit and a friend for life.

I often fantasize about how nice it would be to live back in those good old days. Unfortunately, it's not then, it's now. When the American consumer goes shopping, he or she, often feels that they have been left loose in the middle of a battle zone.

My job in the rest of this chapter is to give you sufficient information, so that you can get in and get out alive and proudly report "Mission accomplished, Sir."

First, let's look at the terrain. There are basically three kinds of appliance stores: The "Mom and Pops;" The flashy Super Store Discount Chains, and the big Department Store Chains.

Sad to say, the "Mom & Pop" is a dying breed. They are smaller than the Super Stores, don't do one tenth the advertising, and are usually a little bit more expensive.

Since my store is one of these, I like to think the small price differential is more than offset by the fact that the sales person usually knows what he or she is talking about and service isn't something that is only done in a foreign country. The fact is that many of these small stores live off their service departments.

The Super Store Discount Chains advertise until most people are totally confused. It's almost all slam, bam price advertising. The prices seem so low that it is hard not to believe they are the only game in town and that you would be silly shopping anywhere else.

The truth is that the prices are not only good, competitive pressures have often forced the retailer to offer prices that are too low to provide the retailer with a legitimate profit on the sale. This forces the retailer and the sales people to get their profit through slick gimmicks and over priced service contracts (more about that in a later chapter).

The low profit structures also often make the sales people slaves to "spiffs." Spiffs" are direct payment from the manufacturer to the sales person for selling specific merchandise. Let me assure you, if the sales person does not make sufficient profit on the sale to support him or herself and his or her family, human nature dictates that he or she will probably do anything short of physical violence to coerce the unsuspecting customer into buying the product on which they will receive a spiff.

You keep hearing horror stories about high pressure salesmanship, super prices on what turn out to be last year's models, and a definite void when it comes to knowledgeable salesmanship.

The big, full service Department Store Chains have been having their own troubles of late. Usually not price competitive with the Super Store Discount Chains, many have de-emphasized, or discontinued, their major appliance departments in the pursuit of a higher profit merchandise mix. Others have forced wage concessions, cutting the salaries, and therefore the ranks, of their professional sales force.

These descriptions are over broad generalities. They do not mean that you will not be hit with high pressure sales tactics at a Mom & Pop, or that some Super Store Discount Chains will not give such superior service that you want to adopt the sales people into your family, or that you might not find the best deal in town on just exactly the appliance you want at the local department store. It just means that you should walk very carefully because there may be land mines out there.

You didn't buy this book for me to soothe you. When you go appliance shopping it is best to be warned. Many distraught customers have described shopping trips to me that are so wild, they have to be lived through to be believed.

The shell shocked customers describe sales people who seem like they are more intent on trying to separate them from their money than give them information they need to make a buying decision. They report receiving glib responses that do not really answer the questions, and a general attitude that implies the customer is stupid for even asking.

During the presentation shoppers are quite often shifted through so many different brands and models that before long everything becomes a blur. Customers become totally confused; and somehow the fantastic low priced appliance that was advertised never seems to be the one they buy.

Any of this sound familiar to you?

At the end of the last chapter I gave you a list of things to do before going appliance shopping. It wasn't First Aid really, it was more like "Preventative Medicine." Here is another batch of tips, things I suggest you do, things I want you to look out for. If you follow these tips, you will be able to go appliance shopping without going through a major life crisis.

How to shop for an appliance

1. Trust in your vibes. If you have followed the directions in Chapter 1, you are going into the appliance store thoroughly prepared. If the sales person greets you with respect, listens to and answers your questions thoroughly, and gives you a feeling of confidence, treat him or her like gold.

If, on the other hand, the sales person talks down to you, shuffles you through a bunch of appliances and a canned sales presentation, gives glib, condescending answers to your questions, fails to show the parts of the equipment you have asked to see, tries to shove a service contract down your throat, fails to give you the respect you feel you deserve as a customer, or does anything else to give you "bad vibes", **get the heck out of there!**

It doesn't matter how much you may have convinced yourself that you could save at that store. I can promise you that those savings are an illusion and you are very lucky if you can get out of the store with your knickers on (Sorry Sister! But it's true, besides the younger generation won't know what I'm talking about anyway.).

2. Be alert for bait and switch advertising and sales techniques. I'll go into this more in a later chapter. For now, if you think you saw the appliance you want advertised at a real low price, then when you go you are told they are temporarily out of that model and can have a rain check, but it won't be in for a month, you are being set up for bait and switch. **Get out of there.**

If the sales person shows you the advertised appliance and then tells you all the reasons why you want a better machine, you are being set up for bait and switch. **Get out of there.**

3. Price is very important. But even if you get the best price in the world from store #1, go through a complete presentation from store #2. Be a little bit flexible. If one store has a super price, but you feel that you are getting superior service at another store and the price is only $25 or $50, be a shooter. The wise shopper should be willing to pay a little more to shop at a store which is perfectly honest and above board and treats the customer like a friend.

4. Beware of service contracts. I have never yet seen a service contract that saved the customer money on a home appliance. On the other hand, I have seen cases where unsuspecting consumers have paid up to $1,800.00 for a service contract they didn't need.

Service contracts may be necessary in the computer industry, or some field where the customer is buying evolving technology. This is not the case in the appliance industry.

Your appliance should not break down, period. If it does, it should break down within the first 90 days. If it does not break down in the first 90 days of use, if you maintain your appliance properly, you should be set for the next seven to ten years!

5. Make sure that the price lists any and all installation costs. Ask what additional parts, if any, may be required to install the machine. If the appliance is delivered and a part that was not listed is required to install the appliance, for which additional parts or labor will be charged, tell the driver or whomever, to put the appliance back in the box and take it back to the store.

6. Do not pay in full up front. I don't care what the store policy is. You can pay a small deposit down if you want to, but **pay in full only after the appliance has been installed, you have inspected it for defects, scratches, etc., and are satisfied that it is the appliance you bought and that it is running well.**

I am confident that if you follow these rules you will be a strong, confident shopper. Nothing I have told you to do will give offense to any honest retailer. So be smart, be strong. Make me proud of you.

Chapter 3

ADVERTISING

One of the guys I play hockey with is always in trouble with women. I will admit at the outset that unlike myself, he is a complete male chauvinist (hockey players tend to be that way). At any rate, one night at the bar as we were imbibing some rejuvenating, fluid replacements after practice, he was complaining that women get furious if you lie to them, yet are impossible to live with if you don't.

I certainly would never, ever, agree with such a remark. However, I will say that it is true when it comes to customers.

Doesn't it seem like half the stores are having half off sales at least half the time? In my neck of the woods, we have a big retail chain that advertises half their products on sale for half off for half the day. Could that not be a case of telling the customer what they think the customer wants to hear?

I've got a simple question for you. Do you think merchandise can really be on sale for one half off more than once or twice a year? As a retailer, this kind of advertising really infuriates me. I know that hard goods retailers buy the majority of their merchandise at 35 to 50% off.

When you add 20% for overhead and 5% for advertising, it is impossible to make more than 10 to 25% when selling the merchandise at full retail. That makes a legitimate 10% off sale a tremendous event.

Would any of you be motivated if a retailer advertised: **Gigantic Sale. Save up to 10%!** Of course not. You would stay away in droves.

But let's take a hard look at the mathematics. If product plus overhead and advertising costs 75 to 90% of retail, then a retailer that advertises 50% off is losing 25 to 40%.

Dear reader, I don't care how big the chain is, volume purchasing will not enable a manufacturer to sell products below cost. No retailer can make any money if they sell merchandise on which they are losing 25 to 40 cents on the dollar.

If this were to be a legitimate sale then one of three things would have to be true:

1. The retailer got the merchandise for free (i.e. **Semour the Super Seller** is a retailer of hot merchandise). I do not believe this for one minute.

2. The retailer is a giant prepared to keep selling merchandise at a loss until they have driven every legitimate competitor out of business, at which time they can jack up their rates and really start giving the public a going over. Ethics aside, I do not think that any retailer has money enough to do this.

3. Somewhere along the way, somebody is fibbing. No, that is too cruel. Let us just say that somewhere along the way, truth is being stretched a little bit to better conform to marketing realities.

How could a retailer do such a thing? Well what if he were able to make a deal with a manufacturer to buy all his excess two and three year old inventory, for maybe 20 cents on the dollar.

Then, he could give the merchandise a double or a triple mark up, cut the price by 50% and still make a handsome profit.

Is it honest? Well according to a pamphlet produced by Esther Shapiro's Consumer Affairs Department, Michigan Public Act 331 of 1976, effective April 1, 1977, prohibited practice #5 is: *"Representing that the goods or services are of a particular standard quality or grade, or that goods are of a particular style or model, if they are another."* [1]

So if the ad says a refrigerator is a 1995 model, when it is a 1993 model, it's illegal, at least in the State of Michigan (most States have similar legislation).

But what if the ad merely says that the refrigerator is "new," or maybe doesn't say anything at all, just that it's a "14 cu. ft. with automatic defroster and automatic ice cube maker." I'm no lawyer, but the ad is probably legal. If it is important to you whether an

---

[1]City of Detroit Consumer Affairs Department, Common Sense, September 1992, 2.

appliance is this year's or some other year's model, finding out that information is up to you.

One good technique is to go to the store and get the Serial Number; then call the manufacturer and find out when that particular machine was made.

You may still decide that it is too good a deal to pass up. But let the Sales Manager know you know the model year. He may decide to give you something extra just to make sure you're a happy customer.

Another technique that retailers, with the active promotion of manufacturers, use to give you the impression that you are making tremendous savings on an appliance, is to advertise a special bare bones, stripped down, version of a popular appliance at a super low price.

You see the price, rush into the store. The salesperson shows you the appliance. He tells you exactly what you will, or will not be getting. He knows that you would not actually buy that appliance on a bet. Nobody would. Then, so you won't have wasted a trip, he shows you a similar appliance, with almost all the bells and whistles, that you could have for just a hundred dollars more.

Is this bait and switch? According to Michigan's Public Act 331 of 1976, prohibited practice #7 is: "*Advertising or representing goods or services with intent not to dispose of those goods or services as advertised or represented."* [2]

According to Esther Shapiro's Consumer Affairs Department that means it's illegal to advertise a low priced appliance with the intent to switch consumers to a higher priced model.

Still, the advertised product is a legitimate product. You are more than welcome to buy it. And the store would be delighted to sell it to you. Soooooooooooooo?

There is no single bad guy in this. What we call "low models" are a pretty close to universal selling technique. These "low models" are quite often featured in big multi retailer, co-op advertising that is sponsored and paid for in large part by the manufacturers.

I once had a low ball priced washer in my store for seven years. I am not talking about a model line, I am talking about a specific washing machine, let's call it Nellie, that I had in my store for seven years.

Nellie was made by one of the finest names in washing machines. Over the seven years she starred in vast number of ads. Consumers would see the ad and come in to my store. Once the lack of features was explained, the customer never wanted to buy Nellie and was usually upgraded to another machine.

---

[2]Ibid.

Hockey is a rough, tough sport, and I've done my share of checking and high sticking. But I have never done anything, before or since, that felt as wrong as my affair with Nellie.

I finally got so ashamed about having Nellie in my store that I sent her back to the manufacturer and stopped participating in the co-op advertising campaign.

What's the reason for telling you this? To make certain you understand that there are a lot of traps and pitfalls out there. Don't believe everything you read in the papers, hear on the radio or see on TV.

Remember, just like my hockey player friend who lamented about having to lie to the ladies and getting in trouble for it, it is not all the manufacturers and retailers fault. Their policies reflect what they believe it takes to move you. In other words, what they think you want to hear.

How can we solve this dilemma? The only way is to get manufacturers, retailers and consumers together. Retailers and manufacturers have to agree to honesty not hype in advertising. Consumers have to get realistic and not expect retailers to sell products at prices that would drive them into bankruptcy.

Chapter 4

SERVICE

I could spend the next ten years writing about the service industry. All I would get is heart burn. All you would get is bored.

The primary purposes for this chapter is: 1, to educate the reader on how to buy service; and 2, to expose enough of the dirty tricks of the trade, so that the good guys in the service industry (and there are many of them) say "enough is enough" and do a better job of protecting the consumer.

There are many scary stories out there. My very good friend, Esther Shapiro, the long time, nationally honored, Director of the Detroit Consumer Affairs Department, has called me in on consumer fraud cases many times. I have had the privilege of appearing at court as an expert witness on many occasions.

In April of 1992, there was as program on the ABC Television Network that said that the consumer had a 50% chance of being ripped off by the service man who came into their home and repaired an appliance. I think their estimate was low.

Buying a major appliance is like taping a "Kick Me" sign on your fanny. Eventually someone is going to avail themselves of the opportunity.

When you start out with a service contract you are surrendering to the inevitable. You have decided that you are going to get worked over on service, and it might as well be by that nice man or woman who sold you the appliance.

Paying for service that you may never need is your prerogative. The only problem is, that if your appliance runs well through the initial warranty period, the probabilities are that you will not have a major service call until after your service contract has expired. So buying a service contract is usually like buying a guarantee that you will pay more than you need on appliance repair.

Don't believe me? Let's compare paying for service as you need it, VS a service contract.

Service VS Service contract

When you buy service as you need it from a service company you pay for the cost of the parts, the cost of the technician's time, truck, tools and equipment, advertising, overhead, and a profit for the company.

When you buy service through a national warranty company you pay for the cost of the parts, the cost of the technician's time, truck tools and equipment, overhead, a profit for the company **plus a**

commission for the salesman, a profit for the store (sometimes the only profit on the appliance because there may be none in the selling price) **the cost of administering the warranty, warranty company overhead, plus a profit for the warranty company.**

Which has to cost you more?

Some may say that the big companies have tremendous economies of scale and make up their costs in volume. If the playing field is equal, a service repair person can only do so much quality work in a 40 hour week no matter for whom he works.

When a big company hires him as an independent contractor and gets his bid down to the lowest possible dollar, it just means the worker has to run from job to job. He doesn't have time to be thorough or make explanations to the consumer. Quality is the first casualty in this kind of an environment.

Why do people buy service contracts?

I believe there are two reasons why people buy service contracts on appliances: **pressure and fear.**

When you buy an appliance you are often pressured by the salesman to buy a service contract. It gets so bad that at some stores the salesman even makes you sign a rejection form saying that you have been offered a warranty extension and declined it.

There are good reasons for all this pressure. Often a large amount of the sales person's income is derived from commissions on service contracts. He or she is in danger of being fired if they do not convert a high enough percentage of appliance sales to service contracts. At some stores, selling prices are so close to cost, that just about the only place store management can look for profit dollars is by selling service contracts.

If you are like most of us, you are a sitting target for this pressure because you have a tremendous fear of having to get service on your appliance. Appliance service repairmen, politicians and used car salesmen run neck and neck in the public trust department.

Many people buy service contracts because they are afraid of not being able to find a good, honest service person when they need one.

I once met a senior citizen who had paid over $1,800.00 on a service contract for an appliance. They had pressured him into paying several times the purchase price of the appliance for service he might never need.

When you buy a service contract you are really betting that you bought shoddy merchandise. If this is the case you would be money ahead investing the money you are willing to put into a service contract into the purchase of a better made appliance. Quality never costs, it saves.

Finding a good appliance repair person need not be a problem. If you shopped for an appliance the way I suggested in Chapter One, you would have already contacted two or three independent service companies and asked them which brands they repaired the least.

One of the people you talked to was probably head and shoulders above the rest. He gave you honest answers and went out of his way to help you at no profit to himself. If I were looking for service, he would be the first that I would consider.

I'd also ask all my friends and relatives if they had a service problem and found a good company. Keep in mind that not every consumer is alike. A friend or relative might have gotten good service and paid through the nose without even knowing. When you get a referral from friends or family, try to find out a little bit about the prices they paid.

The next place I'd consider is the store at which I bought the appliance. After all, if the store has a service department, they will be doing all the repair work while the appliance is under warranty. They should be experts on the product.

Unfortunately, some of the major stores have a couple of extra tiers of costs and profit added to their charges and are not competitive to open market prices.

How to let your fingers "do the walking" without breaking a leg.

The next obvious place to shop is the *Yellow Pages*. Wow! What a frightening thought.

In most *Yellow Pages* there is page after page of ads on Appliance Service and Repair. The more you look, the more you see. Look under Appliance Repair, then under the different appliances by name, Washers, Dryers, Refrigerators, Ranges, Dishwashers, Microwave Ovens and Parts & Service.

All those topics have listings. There are many of the same ads in almost every section. If you look in the Yellow *Pages* for the surrounding communities, surprise of surprises, you'll find most of the same ads there. In Detroit, there are nine different Yellow *Pages* in the major market area. Most of the same companies advertise in all of them!

Many of these companies seem big and powerful. They have big ads... some full pages... some two and three color. They have office phones all over town. They have the names or symbols of the major appliance manufacturers. Some even offer a free service call, if you decide to have the appliance repaired by them. What could be fairer?

Advertising can sometimes be very deceptive.

Always remember the customer, not the business, pays for the advertising. The bigger the ads, the higher the advertising cost. Have you got any idea of the expense involved in running multiple, large ads in many telephone books?

I once talked to one of the real big hitters in the national service industry. He told me that he spent a million dollars a year in the *Yellow Pages*. I already told you he was a biggie, but even the biggest service organizations are not Fortune 500, or even Fortune 5,000 companies. For the most part they are comparatively small business people.

Can you imagine the pressure on a relatively small businessman or woman if they have convinced themselves that they have to come up with a million dollars a year? Even a quarter of that is still $250,000.00. A hundred thousand dollars is more than the cost of most Americans' houses. In a single year! I can tell you very honestly that I could not sleep nights with that kind of pressure.

There are some companies that live up to their ads. But how is the consumer supposed to know which is which?

Quite often it is not what the ads say, but what they imply that is deceptive. Let's look at just three of the ways an unwary consumer can get hooked.

Local Phone Numbers.

Local phone numbers provide a legitimate consumer benefit. You can call a company clear across town, or in the next county, and not be charged for an out of zone call. It saves you money.

However, the local phone number gives the impression that the office is near you. When you see several phone numbers with captions like: North Side, South Side, East Side, you think: "These guys have offices all over town. They must be big and successful."

Quite often this is not the case. I have known business people with phone numbers all over town who only had one office. Convenient when you make the call, but a real aggravation when you have a complaint and have to drive across town to get action.

Manufacturers Names and Logos.

When you see these famous, highly advertised, national names and symbols, the implication is that the service company is a factory authorized repair center. That is, and should be, a real confidence builder.

In the real world, many repair companies listing the top national brands are not only not factory authorized repair centers, they do not even have the national company's permission to use their names or symbols in their advertising. The national company may not even know they exist.

All it takes for an unscrupulous person to include a national company's name in an ad is to include it in the copy when they give it to the advertising sales person.

Free service calls.

Nothing but a puppy's love is free. An ad that indicates that if you have your product repaired by the service firm after they have diagnosed the problem they will not charge for the service call or the travel cost, simply means that they have loaded these charges into their repair costs.

To my knowledge, the cost of the service vehicle, fuel, insurance, tools and equipment, the technician's hourly wage and uniform have never been paid by the Tooth Fairy. No matter what the ad says, these costs have to be factored into every service call. Somebody has to pay for them some time, or the company will go out of business.

That "somebody" is always the consumer.

It would be nice to think that the publishers of the *Yellow Pages* would protect us from advertising that is not perfectly honest and above board. But let's get real. It's a cold, cruel world out there. The people responsible for policing the ads are the same people who sell them.

Can you, or I, or anyone, expect a commission sales person to be a consumer advocate? He or she is paid to sell more ad pages not tell business owners that they should limit their advertising.

As far as multiple local numbers are concerned, the more phone lines a company has, the bigger the phone bill, the more money paid the phone company. The last I heard, the telephone company's stockholders wanted the company to sell more phone lines, so they could make more money.

There are good honest companies in the *Yellow Pages*, a lot of them. The *Yellow Pages* people try to provide a good professional service, but.....but remember, when you let your fingers do the walking, you have to make sure they walk with care.

The Phone Call

When you call the company, the treatment you receive is a good indication of the character of the company. When you call a company for a service call you may get an unresponsive type who has difficulty even taking your name.

If this is what they have on the phone can you imagine the Neanderthal they might send into your home?

The company might have a nice, bright, perky person on the phone who is great on the PR and getting your name and address, but is a real No Nothing when it comes to talking about your needs.

Or you might talk to somebody who instantly understands your problem, asks some intelligent questions, then suggests you try a thing or two to see if you could fix the difficulty yourself and save the money.

Who would you prefer made the service call?

• When you make the call to the service company, keep in mind the telephone is a two way instrument. At the same time you are sizing them up, they are sizing you up. Your demeanor can make a big difference in the cost of the service call. If you act tough, rough and rude on the call, or in person, a professional service technician may follow the adage, "don't get mad, get even."

- Ask what the charge of a service call is. You want a complete explanation. Does the company charge for service calls; or is there a basic minimum? What is their charge for travel time? Does the company make a flat charge per job, or will they charge by the hour and break the time down in fifteen minute intervals?

- Ask if the company has insurance. You want to know about product liability, property damage, bonding and workers' compensation.

Your Homeowners Policy should cover you. But it is always better to be safe than sorry. Tell them to bring a copy of the insurance certificate with them when they come.

- Before making the appointment, it would also be nice if you called the Better Business Bureau and the Attorney General's Office to see if the company you have selected has any black marks against them. But if your dishwasher is broken and there are already two inches of water on the kitchen floor, you may be forgiven for ignoring some of the niceties.

The service call

Preparation for the service call is important.

- Always keep the paperwork on your major appliances in a convenient spot. Find out what the warranty is before the appointment. If the appliance is still under warranty you want to know about it. Look at the warranty carefully. You may be eligible for at least a partial payment on the parts.

- When the technician gets to your home check the warranty with him or her. The technician may know of a warranty extension or recall of which you never heard.

- If the appliance is under warranty, make sure the technician knows that you know about it. More service people than I like to admit, will ignore the warranty if they think they can get away with it. Manufacturers pay a much lower rate for warranty work than you would be charged for regular service. It may not be ethical, or even legal, but we're talking pay checks here. If the mortgage is due, and the week's income has been low, the temptation is to charge the higher amount.

- Don't get dressed up to see the technician. Many service people have been trained by their companies to evaluate your financial condition by your appearance and the looks of your house. The better you look the bigger the fee may be.

- Show the technician the problem, then sit down and watch while he or she decides what the solution is. Don't give the service person the third degree treatment, but ask for an explanation of what he or she wants to do.

If you give the go ahead, sit back down and enjoy the show. A good, honest person will not mind. The technician will enjoy showing off his or her expertise and you may learn enough to make the same repair yourself next time.

A dishonest person could easily cost you a couple extra hundred extra dollars in bogus charges.

- Oh, one thing more. These people are guests in your home, you invited them, be gracious. A technician has a hard job. He or she deserves your respect. Every good tech has my admiration.

- Send someone to look at the service vehicle while you are with the service person. A company which advertises that they carry a full assortment of parts in the truck should verify this in your driveway. If they advertised a full parts inventory and the truck is empty, they lied to you. You may be being set up for a scam. Ask them to leave.

- If the technician seems competent and gives you a choice, you are usually money ahead paying a service or diagnostic charge, plus parts and an hourly charge broken down in fifteen minutes intervals.

This could mount up to a big savings when compared to a flat fee. Flat fees are based on a relatively slow output plus a guaranteed profit. A good technician works much faster than the job is rated.

For instance, say replacing the water valve on a washing machine has a flat job rate of $125.00. A good technician can usually replace that valve in fifteen minutes after he knows the problem.

Opening up the washer is covered under the diagnostic fee. So if the part costs $20.00; fifteen minutes of labor costs $20.00 and there is a $50.00 service call charge, your total cost would be only $90.00. You would have saved $35.00 by paying hourly and not a flat fee.

Naturally, if something goes seriously wrong, you could get charged for several additional hours. There is no free lunch. You are ahead with an hourly charge. Time costs money. If the technician were not working on your job, he or she could be making money repairing someone else's appliance.

When a service man or woman knows they are going to lose money on a job, they are tempted to cut every possible corner and cut their losses. Their service short cuts could add up to even bigger repair bills later.

- When parts are replaced, try to make certain that the parts being installed are new unless you specifically approved the use of used parts.

- When the repair is completed, keep the old parts. Do not allow the technician to take the old parts with them. Watch carefully. A bad guy will try to ruin a replaced part before he leaves it with you. If fraud did take place, you'll want the old parts as evidence.

Last year I interviewed a serviceman who had scammed customers for years. He told me that when he found a broken wire in the mechanical part of a washing machine, he would quote a price of $180.00 for replacing the motor. Then he would yank the old motor out and take it to his truck, dust it off and put it in a box.

A few minutes later, he would bring the new/old motor back to the house, reinstall the motor and fix the wire. Presto! The washer was fixed and he walked out of the house $180.00 richer.

The service man told me he got away with this scam for six years. He never got caught. The only reason he stopped was that his conscience caught up with him. He quit working for the scam experts and started working for an honest firm.

You do not have to be a genius to stop this sort of thing. You don't have to even understand what the technician is doing. Just sit there, keep awake and keep watching.

A bad guy will not take the chance that you know what he is doing. His greatest enemy is an aware consumer. If you're on the lookout, he will do the repair as quickly as possible and go on to someone not as smart as you.

One last word. I do not want to bad rap the entire service industry. Many fine service people are working with me to stop the few bad apples that are ruining the reputation of our entire industry. Regional service organizations on the East Coast and Midwest are debating the ethics of flat fee service calls. These are good signs. The rules could change in consumers' favor.

When you find a good service company, treat the people like gold. Recommend them to friends. Be loud with your praise. Good works always come back to you.

Chapter 5

PLASTIC DRYER VENT LINES

This could be your home.

THERE'S A KILLER

IN YOUR LAUNDRY ROOM

I want you to take a careful look at this picture. If you have a slinky plastic or vinyl dryer vent line on your dryer, this could very easily be your house. Every year there are over 13,000 dryer fires. These fires devastate families. They not only destroy houses, they cause an untold number of deaths and personal injuries due to fire and smoke inhalation.

I am convinced that many, perhaps even the majority of these fires are directly, or indirectly, attributable to flammable, plastic and vinyl vent lines. Because of the fire hazard these vent lines represent, they have already been outlawed by the Canadian Government.

Working with the Joint Fire Counsel and concerned legislators we have

This could be your dryer

revised the building codes and it is now illegal for plastic vent lines to be installed in new or renovated housing in the State of Michigan.[1]

Unfortunately, this is not the case in most other states. Even in the State of Michigan it is perfectly legal for retailers to sell plastic or vinyl vent lines. You just aren't supposed to use the stuff.

---

[1]Construction Code Authority, Inc., "Construction Code Changes," Lapeer, MI, November 7, 1991.

The purpose of this chapter is to do everything in my power to bring the danger of slinky plastic and vinyl dryer vent lines to the attention of the public and legislators throughout the United States.

When I discovered this problem, I had no intent to become a civic crusader. I had a small appliance store and repair business in Garden City, Michigan. An unusual fact kept creeping up: almost all gas and electric clothes dryers upon which we were called to perform service had, you guessed it, slinky plastic or vinyl vent lines.

This seemed so unusual that I began doing some testing in my workshop and confirmed my hypothesis. Unlike rigid metal vent lines, slinky vent lines collect lint in ridge pockets restricting air movement to the outside. This decreases the effectiveness of the dryer, increases strain on the dryer motor, and can eventually cause an extreme fire hazard.

Keep in mind, I am not a Ph.D.. I do not have a million dollar laboratory, and I am not supported by university or government research grants. I am a very blue collar working man who found a danger lurking in the majority of homes in the country and tried to do something about it.

I contacted Underwriters Laboratories, Inc. and the Product Safety Commission is Washington, DC. Both of these fine organizations worked with me and confirmed my findings. An Underwriters

Laboratories, Inc. ruling of July 15, 1987, states that "for dryer installation only rigid or flexible metal duct should be used for exhausting."[2]

I became a man with a mission giving my findings to newspapers, radio and television, church groups, anyone who would listen. I sent letters outlining my findings to the vent line manufacturers, to washer manufacturers. I begged the plastic industry leaders to at least debate me on the subject. No one did.

Over the years I have been in direct contact with fire investigators and fire chiefs throughout the United States and Canada. None have refuted my findings. After investigation, the Chairman of the Michigan Joint Fire Council, summarized it very well in a letter to Henry Green, Executive Director of Michigan's Bureau of Construction Codes:

"The Underwriters Laboratories have withdrawn their listing for using flexible duct for clothes dryers. The manufacturers direct in their installation papers that the use of flexible duct can void the warranty on the unit.

"In view of the above the Michigan Joint Fire Service Council has directed me to write to you this letter asking that your office take a stand to prohibit the use of flexible clothes dryer duct. We further ask that the State Construction Code be amended to prohibit their use."[3]

---

[2]Whirlpool Corporation, Service Pointer #787976 L-216, November, 1987.

[3]R. Sinclair, Chairman, Michigan Joint Fire Service Council letter to Mr. Henry L. Green, Executive Director, Bureau of Construction Codes, Michigan Dept. of Labor, April 8, 1991.

In order to understand why plastic and vinyl dryer vent lines represent such a danger, you have to understand that we are talking about a multi- million dollar industry with an unsafe product that has been installed on 90% of the dryers throughout the country.

Dryer manufacturers know that slinky plastic and vinyl vent lines can cause big problems and direct that they not be used on their products.

The Whirlpool Corporation says: "Nonmetal duct will kink, cause lint buildup within the exhaust system, reduce airflow and create service problems for the dryer. Many heat element failures are caused by restricted exhaust systems.[4]

Maytag is even more to the point. They simply say: "NEVER USE PLASTIC OR NONMETAL FLEXIBLE DUCT.[5]

If you have a plastic or vinyl slinky vent line, the clock is ticking. After years in the service industry, inspecting and repairing dryers, speaking with homeowners, and inspecting homes after dryer fires have taken place, this is what I believe happens. Keep in mind, this could happen to your dryer and your home.

[4]Whirlpool, 1
[5]Matag Installation Instructions, #3-15288

Slinky vent line showing ridges

Slinky plastic and vinyl vent lines are constructed with accordion style ridges. These ridges act like traps collecting lint that should pass through the vent line. This lint begins to build up in the pockets of the vent tubing.

Air becomes more restricted, making it harder and harder for the dryer to do its job. As air is more and more restricted there is a gradual buildup of lint in the dryer housing. If you are very lucky this overwork causes the dryer motor to over heat and you shell out money for an expensive service call .

If you are unlucky, the dryer keeps functioning under increasing strain. In the worst case scenario, the lint buildup in the pockets of the dryer vent becomes bone dry tinder waiting for the slightest spark or flame to become a catastrophe, destroying the dryer and sending flames around the home's laundry room, into the walls, floors, ceilings and rafters.

Feeling better? Remember the chances are nine out of ten that this could happen in your home.

Today, every dryer manufacturer, every fire insurance company, and every appliance service organization in the country knows about the danger slinky dryer vent lines represent in the home.

Major manufacturers have been alerting their installers for the past few years that only rigid metal should be used for dryer venting.

A half hearted effort to come to terms with the problem has been made with the introduction of slinky vent lines covered with aluminum foil rather than plastic or vinyl. I do not believe this solves the major problem. Although the lines are not flammable, the slinky wire ribbing continues to form pockets in the venting which collects lint, forming a major fire hazard.

Presently there are four different types of vent lines manufactured for your dryer: slinky plastic or vinyl; slinky aluminum; flexible ribbed metal; and rigid metal. The first two, slinky vinyl and slinky aluminum foil covered, are prohibited by most manufacturers, and are outlawed for use in Canada and the State of Michigan.

NOT APPROVED BY MANUFACTURERS:

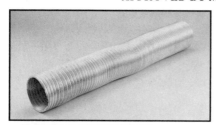

SLINKY VINYL

SLINKY ALUMINUM

APPROVED BY MANUFACTURERS

FLEXIBLE SOLID METAL

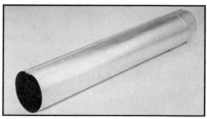

RIGID METAL

Flexible metal and rigid metal are the only two types of vent lines that are authorized by most manufacturers. If you have an equipment failure while the dryer is under warranty and the factory authorized service technician sees a slinky plastic or foil covered vent line attached to the dryer, it may void the warranty and you could be out the price of the dryer.

And that's the easy part. Over the course of years of use, the slinky vent line may clog and may catch fire. You could lose your house and your family.

Although flexible metal vent lines are authorized and are necessary for some installations, I believe the ribbing may eventually cause a limited amount of lint pocket problems. If it is necessary for you to have this type of installation, I recommend that you inspect and clean it at regular intervals to assure that internal lint build up is kept to a minimum.

Rigid metal are the only vent lines I recommend and install. Their smooth inner surface provides the least opportunity for lint build up. Yet, even with the best, when you take your dryer vent down for its annual cleaning, you will be amazed at the amount of lint that has collected over the year.

What can you do to protect your home?

Nothing could be simpler. You can solve the problem yourself in 45 minutes to an hour.

Take my advice and go to your dryer right now and see if you have a rigid metal or a slinky plastic or vinyl vent line. If it is slinky, tear it out.

How to install rigid metal vent line.

Measure the distance between the dryer and the vent. The length of the run should not be more than fourteen feet. Check to see whether your dryer vent pipe is three or four inches. It should be four inches. If your drier has a four inch vent pipe and you adapt it to a three inch diameter vent line, you can cause dryer malfunction. A four inch diameter vent line should be installed.

Go to the store and get enough rigid metal aluminum vent pipe to reach the length of the run. You will also need two adjustable galvanized elbows, one for the dryer, one for the vent opening.

You will probably have to trim one of the vents pipes. Most people can cut the aluminum with a pair of scissors. You will also need some aluminum duct tape.

When you get home, assemble the vent line and make certain your measurements were correct. Then cut the one piece of pipe to size. Assemble the vent line attach it to the dryer vent and exterior vent opening with the adjustable elbows.

It is also a good idea to open the dryer and vacuum up the accumulated lint, and sometimes even cloth, that has become trapped inside the dryer housing.

See how easy it is? That is all that it takes to make a home safe from a dryer vent fire.

Now, take the next step, tell your friends and neighbors about the problem. Call the retailer where you bought your dryer and demand they stop installing slinky dryer vent lines. Rigid metal vent lines only take about ten minutes longer to install and they could save lives.

Call the manufacturer of your dryer and ask what they are doing to stop the installation of slinky plastic or vinyl dryer vent lines. Ask them to include a warning in their advertising and direct rigid metal construction in their installation manuals.

Tell the manager of your local hardware and building supply stores that they should not display slinky plastic and vinyl dryer vent lines because they are a fire hazard.

If we all get together, we can stop dryer vent fires. But remember, if you are like 90% of the people, you have a slinky plastic or vinyl dryer vent in your own home. The problem, and the solution start with you.

Chapter 6

REFRIGERATOR / FREEZER

PART I: SHOPPING?

FIVE QUICK QUESTIONS TO ASK:

1. Could you explain the Energy Guide label to me?

2. Are the doors reversible?

3. Can I add an Ice Maker later?

4. Is there a Power Saver Switch?

5. Please explain the Warranty. Where do I get service?

FIVE QUALITY FEATURES TO LOOK FOR.

1. **Large Crisper Drawers.** You need a lot of room here for all those vegetables, etc.

2. **Solid Door Bars.** Flimsy door bars are the first outward sign of cheap construction.

3. **Large Inner Door Storage Space.** You need lots of room for every day items you need to get to constantly.

4. **Shelves in Freezer Section.** Without shelves you will have to move everything every time you are looking for something for dinner.

5. **Meat Keeper Drawer and Adjustable Shelves.** The meat keeper shelf keeps meat at the proper temperature. Adjustable shelves let you lay out the refrigerator to match your needs.

THINGS TO THINK ABOUT

Your Refrigerator/Freezer is designed to preserve your food in two ways: 1: Freeze it in the Freezer; 2: Keep it cool in the Cooler. Anything else that it does, complicates its life and adds to the cost of the initial appliance, it's upkeep and its eventual repair.

The best suggestion when deciding which appliance to buy is to keep it simple. Automatic ice makers and cold water dispensers are nice. They are also among the most often repaired items on your refrigerator. The average refrigerator is meant to last for 12 to 14 years. Some more, some less.

An automatic ice maker, on the other hand, has a projected life expectancy of only 5.7 years. In other words, you may have to replace, not repair, your ice maker twice before your refrigerator starts to go bad. Replacing an Automatic Ice Cube Maker costs around $150.00 in 1993 dollars. So when you are comparison shopping, add $300.00 to the price of the machine with the Automatic Ice Cube Maker, then compare it to the more simple appliance. How much is the extra convenience worth to you in dollars and cents? Which is the best deal now? You decide.

Ditto for the Cold Water Dispenser.

HOW BIG A REFRIGERATOR DO YOU NEED?

Is your present refrigerator too big, or too small? Industry figures tell us that the average 1 person household needs 10 cubic feet of cooler space and 4 cubic feet of freezer space. You may need more or less. Here's a chart that shows freezer and cooler capacity recommended for various size households.

Each cubic foot of Freezer Space will hold 35 Pounds.

No. Persons in House	-Cubic Feet-		Total
	in Cooler	in Freezer	
1	10	4	14
2	12	4	16
3	14	4	18
4 - 5	16	6	22
6 - 8	16	10	26
9 - 10	17	10	27

WHAT ARE THE MOST POPULAR FEATURES?

This information is just to let you know approximately what percentage of people are buying a certain feature. This is not a recommendation as to what you should buy. The projections are estimates based on retailers' sales.

Popular Refrigerator Features	
Category	**Unit Sales**
Basic 20%	
Frost Free 80%	
Side by Side 33%	
Over/Under 67%	
With Ice Cube Maker 17%	
With Cold Water Dispenser 12%	

WHO'S ON TOP?

The following market share estimates are presented because I thought you might like to know who makes the most refrigerators. They are based on an exclusive survey by *Appliance Manufacturer* magazine. Keep in mind that market share is just one of many factors you should consider. Limited market share does not mean low quality.

1992 Refrigerator Market Share[1]		
Approximately 7,568,000 total units.		
Make	**Ownership**	**Market Share**
GE	GE	36%
Whirlpool	Whirlpool	27%
WCI	Electrolux	19%
Amana	Raytheon	9%
Admiral	Maytag	7%

[1]*Appliance Manufacturer*, February 1993, 18.

SHOPPING TIPS:

A Refrigerator / Freezer is basically just two cold boxes standing side by side or piled one on top of the other, a very simple machine. Therefore simple to shop for. Here are a few things to consider when you comparison shop.

Energy Efficiency. Refrigerators and freezers are the only two major appliances in your home that run 24 hours a day, 365 days a year. Energy efficiency is therefore very important. Compare the Annual operating costs of the appliances. Don't take the Energy Usage Decals for granted. Bring a small calculator with you. Multiply the average energy usage per hour of the machine by 8,760 (the number of hours in the year). Multiply this number by the kilowatt hour cost in your community. That amount should be on your electric bill, or call your power company and they will tell you.

Reversible Doors. If you are shopping for a top mounted refrigerator, make sure that the model you select has reversible doors. If it is more convenient for you to open the refrigerator door from the right than the left, the retailer will usually be able to do this for you before, or at delivery.

If you ever move the appliance to a new location where it would be convenient to reverse the way the door opens, it is a simple D-I-Y project. You will find the instructions in your manual.

Repair & Replacement Costs. Now, compare repair and replacement costs. My motto is "No Surprises!". The more you know before you buy, the better selection you will make. The three parts that have to be replaced most often on a refrigerator are: The Defrost Timer; the Defrost Heater; and the Fan Motor-Freezer

If the appliance retailer at which you are shopping has a parts department. Check out the retail costs of these parts at your retailer. If the retailer does not have a parts & service department, ask a service company.

Part #1: The Defrost Timer

A Clock which shuts off the compressor and sends current to the heater. This part can fail at any time and has an average 6 year life. The part costs around $35.00. The service call and labor ranges between $70.00 and $125.00.

Part #2: The Defrost Heater

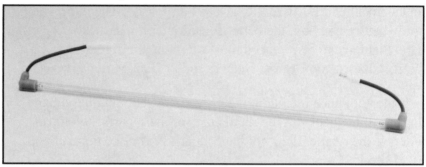

The Defrost Heater melts the "snow" accumulation on the Evaporator Coil. This part can fail at any time and has an average 6 year life. The part costs between $25.00 and $75.00. Add another $75.00 to $125.00 for the service call and labor.

Part #3 The Freezer Fan Motor

The Freezer Fan Motor moves air throughout both the Refrigerator and the Freezer Sections. This part can fail at any time and has an average 6 year life. This part ranges between $25.00 and $40.00. Add another $75.00 to $125.00 for the service call and labor.

Just as the retail prices for the various refrigerator/ freezers differ, so do the prices of their replacement parts. When you add replacement part cost into the cost of the equipment over the life of the machine, you may get an entirely different buying equation. My advice, check out the cost of part replacement in your area before you buy. You will be amazed at how this can effect your true cost during the life of the appliance.

PART II: SETUP:

Believe it or not, location can affect refrigerator repair and maintenance costs by as much as 50%. As a refrigerator creates **cold** its motor creates **heat**. Its a viscous cycle. The hotter the outside temperature, the harder the mechanical parts of the refrigerator have to work to keep the inside cool.

The harder the mechanical parts work, the more heat they create. The harder and hotter the equipment runs, the shorter the life expectancy of the unit.

If you want your refrigerator / freezer to last a long time, it is important to place it in a spot where it gets plenty of ventilation and is away from other sources of heat. Here are some "do's and don'ts."

Do's

Do make sure there is a free flow of air around the refrigerator. The refrigerator is air cooled. If enough air doesn't circulate properly, overheating and premature burnout will occur.

Do make sure the refrigerator is positioned almost level, with a slight backward tilt (about 10⁰). This will automatically keep the refrigerator doors sealed and prevent the kids from leaving the doors open. You can make the adjustment very easily by adjusting the rollers at the front of the appliance.

Do plug the refrigerator / freezer directly into the main power source, no extension cords. Extension cords are a prime cause of compressor burn out.

Don'ts

Do not jam the refrigerator flat against the wall or tight against other appliances or shelves that can restrict the air flow. Air flow is essential to the proper operation and cooling of the refrigerator condenser motor.

Do not position the refrigerator in a spot where it gets a great deal of sun. The sun's rays add heat, and can bleach the color out of a colorized refrigerator in just a few short years.

Do not place the refrigerator on top of, in back of, or beside a heat source, such as a stove or heating vent. The additional heat can really stress-out the refrigerator motor. The motor has to work twice as hard trying to keep the inside of the Cooler and Freezer at the proper temperature. The motor overheats from over use, burn out occurs, and you will be stuck with a very expensive, but clumsy looking book case.

Do not place the refrigerator on carpet. Carpeting retains heat and makes the compressor run longer and hotter. The hotter and longer the compressor runs, the more energy it consumes and the greater the wear and the higher the probability of compressor burn out. If your kitchen is carpeted, cut out a piece of vinyl or linoleum flooring the size of the undercarriage and slip it under the refrigerator. The linoleum won't show and the appliance will run much cooler. Be careful not to hit the condenser motor fan blade with the linoleum. The fan blade is very fragile and you could cause a great deal of damage.

Do not place the refrigerator on additional rollers. Most refrigerators come with rollers. They have been designed into the equipment. Putting your refrigerator on appliance rollers can interfere with the air flow. Many modern refrigerators and freezers have the condenser located under the product. Appliance rollers can interfere with air flow and/or injure the condenser unit. Non factory appliance rollers can make a refrigerator / freezer easier to move, but often add up to very expensive repair bills.

Do not use an extension cord. Position your refrigerator/ freezer so that it can be plugged directly into the household current. A cheap, thin, long extension cord, can not run sufficient voltage necessary to keep the compressor running. It forces your appliance to run under permanent "brown out" conditions. Voltage starvation is a prime cause of premature compressor burn out.

Sometimes, when your power has been knocked out in a bad storm, it is necessary to get power from a neighbor across the street. Usually this is an invitation to disaster. All electricity is not equal. Your well meaning neighbor may save your meat, but ruin your refrigerator in the process. If you do this, use a heavy duty, three prong power cord. It is usually much better to buy or rent a portable generator and have one or two appliances operating directly from the compressor unit.

Do not store the refrigerator in an area where the temperature will drop below 55° F for an extended period of time. Lower temperatures can ruin the sealed system of the unit.

Do not store the refrigerator on its side. This is especially important when you ship the refrigerator from, let's say the house to the cottage. The cooling system of a refrigerator was designed to be upright. Putting it on its side can destroy the integrity of the unit. You can easily lose the Freon™ and the refrigerator will be worthless.

If you must store the refrigerator in a non-upright position, or, horror or horrors, ship it standing on its side, make certain that you do not accidentally lay the appliance on its back, crushing the condenser coils. Even with the refrigerator- freezer on its side, take special care that there is no pressure on the coils. Bending or breaking here can easily ruin the appliance.

After a refrigerator / freezer has been laid on its side, make certain that it stands upright for at least an hour before plugging it in and turning it on. This allows the oil to migrate back down to the bottom of the compressor. Not waiting, could cause the compressor motor to run hot and burn out.

PART III: MAINTENANCE:

Daily:

1. Check your refrigerator daily to see that you (or whomever else it is convenient to blame) have not covered any shelves with wax paper or aluminum foil. Refrigerator shelves are specially designed to let air circulate. Covering them stops the air from circulating properly and causes "hot pockets" within the cabinet. Bad for food. Bad for the refrigerator.

2. If you see rust developing on metal shelves, it usually means that table salt from the kitchen table or counter top is being tracked in on the bottom of pans and dishes. You must keep the bottom surfaces of stored items clean if you want to keep your refrigerator looking good.

3. Make sure that all the food in the refrigerator is covered. This accomplishes two things. It not only keeps the quality of the food better; it also keeps air born acid from acidic foods, like tomatoes, from being circulated by the blower fan throughout the Cooler. Air born acid attacks the metal evaporator coils. Over a period of time the corrosion caused by the air born acid can ruin the coils and force the purchase of a new refrigerator.

4. Keep the freezer compartment at least half full. If necessary, fill plastic milk jugs 3/4 full with water and freeze them. The reason for this is that during the defrost cycle 60° F heat circulates through the freezer. If you don't have enough bulk in the freezer, food will begin to thaw. Keeping the freezer at least half full eliminates the problem.

5. Fill a plastic cup with water and put it in the freezer. When the water freezes, put a penny on top of the ice and position the glass where you will see it when ever you open the freezer. Check the glass daily. If you ever see the penny disappear, you have a temperature problem, or a thief.

6. Stack food scientifically. Different refrigerators have the motors located in different places. Some in the back. Some underneath the bottom of the compartment. Electric motors give off heat. Temperatures, in even the best of refrigerators, vary greatly.

Never put something that must be kept especially cold, near possible hot spots. It is safest to keep food away from the door, the back and the bottom of the freezer section.

This is very important when you are trying to keep something like ice-cream especially cold. **Never store ice-cream in the door of the freezer compartment.** It will turn soft every time. The best place to locate ice-cream in most refrigerators is midway between front and back on the middle or upper shelf.

QUARTERLY:

1. Clean the condenser coils.

Not cleaning the coils at least quarterly is the prime cause for service calls and compressor burn out.

Don't blame yourself for not knowing this. Nobody ever told you despite the fact that this has been the primary refrigerator problem since they were invented. My hat is off to the Amana Corporation. They have installed a warning light on the front of their large refrigerator which goes on when the condenser needs cleaning.

The condenser coil wires or mesh are located at the back, and or beneath the refrigerator / freezer. The sole purpose of these wires is to radiate heat away from the cooling unit of your appliance. Over the years, dust, dirt, and grime collect around the wires and mesh and act as insulation, effectively stopping the condenser from doing its job.

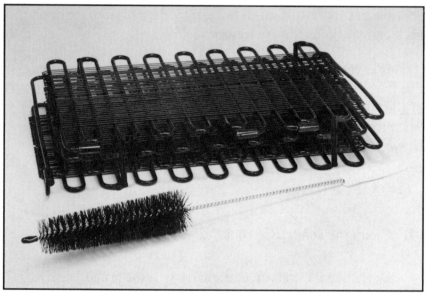

Condenser coils and condenser brush.

Here's how to clean the condenser coils:

1. If you do not have a refrigerator or condenser brush, go out and buy one. It only costs a couple of bucks and you can get it at any good hardware store.

2. Shut off the refrigerator by pulling the plug, or by turning the control to the "OFF" position.

3. Remove the grill at the bottom of the refrigerator and use the condenser brush and the vacuum cleaner hose and crevice

attachment. Clean all the gunk and dust from under the refrigerator. Be careful not to bend the condenser fan blade.

2. Clean drain pan underneath the refrigerator.

This small tray designed to hold the runoff created in self-defrosting refrigerators has to be cleaned with hot soapy water every time you clean the coils. It doesn't matter if it looks dry. The small amount of water from the defrost cycle evaporates rapidly but the dark, moist climate under the refrigerator makes the drain pan the ideal place for bacteria formation. Dr. Shildberg, a good doctor friend of mine tells me that the drain pan is the worst place in the kitchen as far as bacteria is concerned. It is a "hot house" and a definite health hazard.

Many refrigerators also locate blower motors on the under side of the appliance. This blows the bacteria ridden air around the kitchen.

To stop this nonsense, wash the drain pan out in hot, soapy water at least once a month. Use a brush and get into all the corners. Get rid of the calcium deposits left by the evaporating moisture. Rinse and dry the pan and replace. Dr. Shildberg recommends pouring some Hydrogen Peroxide into the pan to kill off the bacteria before replacing.

Drain pans are made of very flimsy materials, therefore they tend to crack easily. If you spring a leak, you usually don't have to replace it. Just line the pan with aluminum foil. This "fix" should last about ten years.

HUMIDITY SWITCH

The humidity switch is called by different names on different makes of refrigerators. Whatever it's called it has one purpose. That is to prevent humidity from forming on the center or edges of the frame of the refrigerator itself.

Every geographic area of the country has one or two humid seasons of the year. When it is humid in your part of the country, turn the humidity switch on to the "On" position. Some people do not do this because they think they are saving money. Wrong. The switch activates a very low wattage heating unit which heats the mullions and combats the formation of humidity.

If you do not turn the humidity switch on during the high humidity season little drops of water form on the center edges of the frame. Over a period of time, these little drops of moisture can rot the refrigerator seals. The humidity heating unit costs just pennies to run and can save you a hundreds of dollars in repair bills. Look for the humidity switch now, if you can't find it, consult your refrigerator manual. Know where it is located and turn it on and off with the change of weather conditions.

When the humidity switch is on, you should be able to feel a little heat when you put your hand on the center mullions. It should feel warm, not hot. If it feels extra hot, this is one of the first signs of failure on your appliance.

ANNUALLY:

1. **Completely clean the condenser area.** At least once every year, disconnect, or turn off the refrigerator and pull it away from the wall. Unscrew the cardboard that protects the condenser coils on the back of the refrigerator and clean the condenser coils, wires, and mesh completely. Clean the dust and grime off the fan blades on the back, but be careful not to bend them. Dust and reattach the cardboard shield. Push the refrigerator back in place.

2. **Clean Door Seals.** While the refrigerator is still unplugged (or turned off), clean the refrigerator's door seals (gaskets) with a 100% cotton rag and a good all purpose organic cleaner and warm water. This is very important to do because door seals on today's refrigerators often cost well over $100.00.

If the cleaning liquid freezes on the door seal, wait a couple of minutes until the seals have reached room temperature and repeat. You want to make certain that those door seams are very clean and supple.

Be especially careful to clean the underside on the bottom of the door seals. This is the most hard to get at, yet is usually the dirtiest. There is no easy way to do this. Open the door, or pull out the drawer, get on your belly and get the water up into the seal. Be sure to get that nice icky area where the seal attaches to the door.

After you have cleaned the door seals carefully, apply a light coat of Vaseline© on the hinge side of the seal. This will keep the seal supple and prevent it from roll over caused by friction every time you open or close the door.

TROUBLE SHOOTING:

PROBLEM: LONG RUNNING TIME OF RE-FRIGERATOR MOTOR.

A person usually becomes aware of the "problem" when they have a new, or recently repaired Refrigerator. Relax. Ninety-five percent of the time this is not a problem. The sounds of our Refrigerators, like all our loyal household servants, usually fade into the background and we are unaware of them.

All of a sudden, because we have suddenly shelled out a bundle of money on our refrigerating unit, an awareness develops in the frontal lobe of our brains and we start actually listening to the sound of the appliance. Lo and behold the motor goes on and on and on. Something must be wrong. Those blankety, blank thieves have taken our money and given us faulty goods.

Chill off folks. When a refrigerator is cooling down, or has just gone through a defrost cycle, it is perfectly normal for the motor to have to run continuously for an hour or more. No problem. There is usually nothing to be concerned about.

If you're still concerned:

The modern refrigerator has two main parts: the cooler and the freezer. To see if your refrigerator is working properly, check to see at what temperature the cooler and the freezer are keeping the food.

COOLER:

The refrigerator should keep your food at about 34 ° to 40° F. Any warmer and food will spoil too fast. Any cooler and the food will run the risk of freezer damage. Notice that I said the temperature of the food, not the temperature of the air inside the refrigerator.

If you have a self-defrosting or frost-free refrigerator, the heater that goes on during the defrosting cycle, may induce as much as 60° F of heat into the appliance during the thaw cycle. After automatic defrost cycle, the fan motor spreads this warm air throughout the cooler and freezer compartments.

An air temperature reading taken during the thaw cycle can therefore be very misleading and tell you nothing about the temperature at which the food is being maintained. This bad reading, could become the basis for your spending many dollars on unnecessary repair costs.

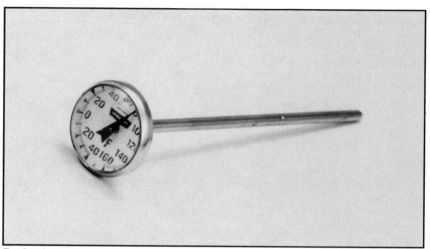

Probe thermometer.

Use a good probe thermometer to check the temperature at which the refrigerator is keeping your food.

To find out how well your refrigerator is functioning, buy a good probe thermometer. Clean the probe thoroughly and then insert it into a jar of something that has been in the refrigerator for at least several hours. The reading should go to 40° F (4.4° C).

Make certain that you get a good probe thermometer (price around $8.00 US. A cheap probe thermometer does not have the necessary sensitivity and can easily be 5° F + or -. That is unacceptable).

Millions of people have been suckered into buying "shelf top" or hanging thermometers especially made for refrigerator use. These measure only air temperature and are not acceptable to you. If you have one, do yourself a favor and **throw it away.**

FREEZER

Now, test the freezer. The freezer should keep your food at about -10° to +10° F (23.2° to -12.2° C). To test this, push the probe thermometer into something soft like ice cream.

GENERAL:

Don't run the temperature test using food located on the bottom of the compartment, near the front or in the door of the cooler or freezer. These areas are always a little warmer and will give you an untrue (and worry inspiring) reading.

If the food temperature is too high in either the cooler or the freezer section, we may have a problem.

Usually this is a sign you have not been maintaining your appliance properly and the temperature problem will mysteriously disappear after you have gone through a complete maintenance cycle. Worst case scenario is changing the door seals. But that is the last thing we do.

First: Completely clean the compressor area as explained under daily maintenance. Folks, this sounds too simple. But every year I save people thousands of dollars in my appliance repair business by simply telling them to do this **before** they pay for a service call. The reason you bought this book was to save money on appliance repair. Trust me.

Second: Check the door seals (gaskets). Do a visual check first. See if any foreign matter (egg yoke, gravy, etc.) has collected on the seal. If they are dirty, that may be your problem. The next step is to check for heat leaks.

PROBLEM: LEAKING AIR SEALS.

The easiest way to check for leaking door seals is to do a light test. This test is best done at dusk or night. Take a flashlight and turn it on. Put it in the refrigerator. Close the refrigerator door. Turn off the lights. Then check all the way around the door seal to see if any light is escaping. If you can not see light, the seal is fine. If you see light, the door is not sealing properly. Test both the cooler and the freezer compartment.

If you see light do not panic. Leaking door seals can usually be fixed very easily. Mark the places around the refrigerator where you can see light with a grease pencil.

Very carefully, heat the seals where they leak with a nozzle type electric hair drier. Be careful not to burn the plastic inner door panel.

As you heat the seal, stretch it with your fingers, until the seal is back to its original shape.

If the seal is torn, get some rubber glue at the hardware store and apply it to the damaged area. If there are actual gaps in the seal, fill in with silicone sealant also available at most hardware stores.

When you have finished and your sealing job is done, let dry, then retest the seal with the flash light. If you no longer see the light, the job is done. If you still see light, build up some more with the rubber glue or Silicone sealant.

Replacing door seal:

If the door seal has deteriorated so badly that it can not be repaired and must be replaced, the job is not as difficult as it may seem. Get the make and model number and check out several different sources on the parts price.

When you pick up the new seal, it will usually have an instruction sheet enclosed in the package. Follow the instructions closely.

Here are a few tips:

1. Take a pencil and draw a line all the way around the existing seal. You want the new seal to conform to the exact same format.

2. Soak the new seal in a sink or tub of hot water for ten or fifteen minutes. This will make it more pliable and easier to work with. Remove the seal from the water. Dry with an old towel.

Sometimes the door seal has magnets in only three sides. If this is the case, be sure that you match up the new seal with the old. If magnets are not on the original sides, the door will not close properly and you will have to take it off and redo the job.

3. You do not have to take the refrigerator door off its hinges to do this. Open the door and flip up the seal with your finger. You will see that the seal is connected by a flap which fits under a strip of metal. The strip of metal, seal flap and inner door liner are all connected to the door by a series of screws. Remove the screws from the top and half way along each side.

4. Gently remove the unscrewed portion of the seal and just let it dangle from the door.

5. Put the new seal in place and attach it on the top and about one third of the way along both sides. Insert the screws, but tighten only enough to hold the seal in place under the metal strip. Do not tighten all the way yet.

6. Remove the remainder of the old seal and screws and attach the new seal along the sides and bottom of the door. Do not over tighten the screws yet.

7. Close the refrigerator door carefully. Observe whether the new seal conforms to the pencil line. Make any necessary adjustments.

8. Now begin to tighten the screws. Work corner to corner and side to side. Start at the top. After you have tightened six screws, two at the upper corners, two at the lower corners, one on each side, close the door gently. Check to see if the seal is seating properly. If not adjust immediately.

9. Repeat the procedure with six more screws, again and again, until the seal is in place.

The tightening procedure is very important because the whole strength of the door is provided by the inner panel being attached to the door vial the door seal. The outer panel is a piece of sheet metal which is very pliable when the screws are loosened.

Sometimes the bottom or top corner of the door gets out of kilter and will no longer seat against the frame properly and has to be aligned before the door will seal properly. Do not panic. Just pretend you are a chiropractor and give the door an "adjustment." This is done by gently twisting the door.

10. If you observe any cracks in the inner plastic door liner, get some plastic mender from the hardware store and patch. Be sure to fix them because a broken or cracked liner can result in a weaker door and will also allow moisture inside the door resulting in rust and corrosion.

Also, if there are any wires or heaters inside the door, this moisture could cause a severe shock hazard.

PROBLEM: REFRIGERATOR ODORS

Odor problems run all the way from the smell you get from accidentally putting uncovered chopped onion into the refrigerator to the disaster you get when rotting food is accidentally stored in a sealed, unplugged appliance sitting out in the garage during the summer. We'll start with the light duty "fixes" and get progressively more aggressive.

I assume that by now everyone knows the old tip of keeping an open box of baking soda in the back of one of the refrigerator shelves. If you don't, stop reading this book right now, go to the cupboard, take out a one pound box of baking soda. Open it and put the box in the refrigerator. Ninety per cent of all odor problems are now eliminated.

More difficult odor problems can be solved with many of the commercial products you can purchase at your local hardware store. Be sure you use something like Smells Be Gone™ or Odor Guard™ that are safe to use around food. These are not "maskers," they are actual "odor eaters" which attack the bacteria that causes the smell. No bacteria, no smell. Simple.

If the odor still persists, you may want to use some of grandmother's recipes: charcoal, coffee grounds, crumpled newspaper. When all else fails you can use the same technique people used to use when their dog got the wrong end of a fight with a skunk.

Empty the refrigerator and wash the cooler and freezer compartments out with 100% pure tomato juice. Let stand for a couple of hours. Then rinse.

If the old tomato bath doesn't work, your options are getting pretty slim. The only other possibility I know is to take the refrigerator outside on a hot sunny day. Open the doors and leave it open to the sun for three days.

Smell still there? If you can't live with it, throw the appliance away. Be sure to take the doors off before you take it to the dump. You do not want any child, or even any animal, getting trapped inside.

Usually, the cause of odor problems such as this is when a large quantity of bloody meat is allowed to go bad in a refrigerator and the spoiled meat juices ran into all the nooks and crannies and between the walls of the appliance. If you run into a problem like this, the only solution is to throw the appliance away.

Mold and mildew smells in stored refrigerators can often be eliminated with a thorough washing, liberal application of a chemical odor eater, and a thorough airing. If the smell is still there, plug in the appliance and let it run for a few days on a cold setting. The thoroughly cold machine often has a much lower scent and may be adequate.

PROBLEM: PLUGGED DRAIN

This is one of the most common causes of service calls. Plugged drains on refrigerators cause the needless expenditure of millions of dollars annually. When your refrigerator goes on to the defrost cycle, frost, little particles of frozen water, accumulates on the evaporator and turns into water.

This water travels down to the drain pan under the refrigerator through an engineered path. At the very bottom of the path is a trap, very similar to the trap under the sink in your house. The trap holds water and prevents hot air from traveling from the warm underside of your refrigerator and into the cooler and freezer compartments of your refrigerator.

Mineral deposits from the water gradually build up and can eventually clog the refrigerator drain.

TOP MOUNTED REFRIGERATOR:

When this occurs on a top mount refrigerator (freezer on top) you will find water under the crisper drawers.

If this occurs, look inside the cooler section up on the ceiling near the back wall. You will find a trough or cup which catches the water during the defrost cycle.

Take a bulb type baster, like you use to baste a turkey, and fill it with hot water. Insert the baster tip into the hole and squeeze the water out into the hole. The stream of hot water floods the drain, melts any frozen particles and clears away the mineral deposits. You just saved yourself a $75.00 service call.

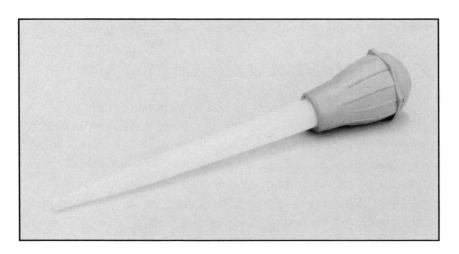

SIDE BY SIDE REFRIGERATOR:

In a side by side refrigerator (freezer and cooler compartments side by side), the trough is located at the very bottom of the freezer compartment against the back wall. Water accumulates at the very bottom of the freezer compartment. Use the same technique described above.

If you can not insert the baster into the drain hole, use a flexible thin plastic hose. Insert one end of the hose in the hole. Then fill your mouth with hot water (careful not to scald your mouth), and blow the hot water through the hose. Make sure you just blow, and take your mouth away from the hose before you inhale. The gunk at the bottom of the drain could make you very sick if you inhale it into your system. Now take the family out to dinner, or do something nice with the $75.00 you just saved on the service call.

PROBLEM: VIBRATING COMPRESSOR

The refrigerator compressor sits on four rubber grommets. Through years of usage the grommets lose their resiliency. The compressor begins to knock against the frame on which it is situated. To test this take a large screwdriver and put it underneath the compressor. This will remove some of the tension on the rubber grommets. When the compressor goes on if the compressor runs more quietly, the problem is the grommets.

The solution is to purchase some new grommets and replace the old. This is a very simple procedure. If you do not want to do that, take a chunk of car tire and ram it under the compressor. The sound will be eliminated.

PROBLEM: ICE MAKER PROBLEMS

ICE CUBES HAVE FOOD ODOR

Ice cubes are one of the first things to pick up stray odor from your refrigerator. Solve the problem by sealing all the smelly things in the cooler in tightly topped jars and dishes. The open box of baking powder in the back of the cooler will help.

ICE CUBES TASTE BAD

Usually this is caused by your drinking water. Attach an in-line filter you can get at the hardware store to the pipe diverting water to the ice cube maker.

ICE CUBE MAKER STOPPED MAKING ICE CUBES.

If the ice cube maker stops making ice, first check to see that the wire arm over the ice cube tray isn't pushed up, shutting off the ice cube delivery. While you're at it check to see that cubes are not wedged into the maker jamming delivery.

If both these systems are "go", go to the back of the refrigerator and check out the power with a 110 volt cord. Hook the 110 Volt cord up to the terminals on the coil. The power should send a stream of water into the ice maker. If it does not, simply replace the water valve and the problem should be solved.

STAND ALONE FREEZERS

SHOPPING TIPS:

The size of the area you have available will play a big part in whether you buy an upright or a chest type freezer. Using the principal that cold air falls when you open a freezer door, I believe a chest type freezer is more efficient. An upright freezer is more convenient. Shelves are handier and less stacking and re-stacking is required.

The number of people in your home and the amount of food you need to freeze should determine the size. Keep in mind that bigger is not always better. You want the freezer to be as close to full as possible at all times. One cubic foot of freezer space will hold up to 35 lbs. of food!

- Shelving is worth its weight in gold. Shelves help you organize the food and find things more easily.

- I don't recommend self defrosting freezers. During the defrost cycle, the heater is sending a stream of 40° F air through the freezer. Some of this heat has to be absorbed by some of the food degrading the taste over a period of time. If you install the freezer properly and use it with respect, you will only have to defrost the freezer two or three times a year. The improved food quality is worth the slight extra work.

- The faster the freezing time, the better. Meat and vegetable packers advertise "Flash Frozen" foods because rapid freezing retains food quality. In practice, slow freezing allows the cell walls in the food to weaken. When the food thaws, cell walls rupture and juices, vitamins and taste escape.

Although there are several very good freezers on the market, the fastest upright residential freezer I know is the Amana which has a cooling coil (evaporator) attached to every shelf, ceiling and back wall. Naturally, the more direct the cooling, the faster the freezing.

- Don't install an ice maker. It will just induce you to open and close the freezer door more often and make the freezer inefficient.

INSTALLATION:

Install the freezer in as cool a location as possible. The less outside heat the freezer has to overcome, the easier it will run.

The more solid and even the floor the better. Due to its great weight, it is essential that a large upright freezer be placed on the most sturdy, level floor possible. The weight creates an imbalance. To check this out, place your hand on the side of the freezer near the top edge of the door opening and push. The freezer will actually move up and down slightly. This proves the imbalance of freezer VS door.

With upright freezers, make certain that the unit is perfectly level from side to side, then raise the front slightly higher than the back to assist the door seal. With chest freezers make sure the freezer is perfectly level from side to side and front to back.

Run the freezer on a separate circuit. Either buy a freezer with a warning light, or put a little night light in the adjoining plug. Monitor the light from time to time to make certain that the freezer is getting power.

MAINTENANCE & USE:

Defrost the freezer according to the instructions in the owners manual.

Store the food with as much uniformity as possible across all shelves. A heavy weight in one section of the freezer can cause the freezer door to shift, ruining the door seal.

Never, I repeat, never, chip away the frost accumulation inside the freezer with a sharp object. It is very natural to want to scrape away the frost build up, like you would scrape the windows of the a car.

Thousands of people do this every year and puncture a hole in the evaporator coil. Once you puncture the coil, there is no repair and you have to buy a new freezer.

Do not speed thawing time with a hair dryer or heat gun. It is not safe to run an electric appliance in the wet atmosphere of a defrosting freezer. The retained heat from the electric hair dryer of heat gun is not dissipated with the melting of the ice. It is retained within the freezer walls and will cause an extreme strain on the cooling unit when it is plugged in.

Chapter 7

ELECTRIC RANGES

PART I: SHOPPING?

FIVE QUICK QUESTIONS TO ASK:

1. **What is the range top made of?** Will it discolor or chip? How easy is it to clean?

2. **Do the burners pull out or are they wired into the stove?** How expensive are they to replace?

3. **Does the cook top lift up for easy cleaning?** What Warranty does it carry?

4. **What is the wattage of the burners?** How fast do they heat?

5. **How expensive are the knobs and elements to replace?**

FIVE QUALITY FEATURES TO LOOK FOR:

1. Simplicity of controls.

2. High Wattage top burners with quick heating elements.

3. Porcelain drip bowls and pop up range top for easy cleaning.

4. Large oven interior with oven light and door glass window for good visibility.

5. Storage drawer for pots and pans.

THINGS TO THINK ABOUT

If I were shopping for an electric range today, the first thing that I would do would be to call the manufacturers of at least three of the major brands and ask them to send some literature. Then, I'd go to the library and research which brands and models were most highly recommended in the consumer research magazines.

During my research I'd pay special attention to the following: What cooking and convenience features offered by the manufacturer make him stand out?

How do the size and appearance of the various models fit my kitchen?

What different styles of burners does the manufacturer offer?

Are the knob locations and other safety factors designed with children, especially toddlers, in mind?

Finally, what is the capacity of the storage drawer? Has it been designed to be valuable space I will use, or just fill a hole?

When I was fairly close to making a decision on which I wanted, I'd find a friend or neighbor who had the make and model I was interested in and find out exactly what she or he thought of the product of my choice.

You'll find that choosing a range today is a difficult proposition. All the leading products have beautifully engineered features designed to make life easier. The more you read about them, the more entranced you get. Soon you want a range with every feature on the list. You, the homemaker (whether male or female), have to be pleased. This is an appliance that you are going to use daily. Be practical, but don't scrimp. If you don't get what you want, you'll be an unhappy camper for the next fifteen years and the entire family will suffer.

That means that you should read what I say in the next few paragraphs and then go out and do what ever you want. The most important thing about a range is that the chef is happy. Everything else, including my words of wisdom and practicality, is secondary.

One feature you have to look out for is size. It may be that stoves are getting to be like men's ties. Back in the 1950's the ranges were 40" wide. In the 1960's the manufacturers stopped making that width and started making ranges 30" wide. Thousands of Americans had to remake their kitchen counters or be stuck with 10" of dead space next to their stove.

Now, the scuttle butt is that the manufacturers are going back to 40" widths. This should make the kitchen remodelers very happy but it is going to be very expensive for the rest of us.

Here are a few drawbacks to some of the most popular features:

• Smooth top ranges look beautiful. But you really have to be a cleaning fanatic to live happily. Everything makes a mess.

• Burners that turn up, instead of pull out for cleaning can be a problem. The burners that just turn up for cleaning are soldered. If a soldered burner burns out, you have a big service charge. If a pull out burner burns out, you pull it out, go to the store, and replace it.

- Manual clean ovens are very practical. They are cheaper to buy and have less to go wrong. However, they are a time consuming mess to clean.

- Continuous clean ovens have a rough textured surface which resists stains for a short time. After a couple of years they look dirty all the time and you will start making excuses to keep a helpful guest from putting something into the oven.

As a consumer advocate this is one of the features that really gripes me because usually only the most fastidious (read practically perfect) people will buy ranges with the continuous clean feature, then they are stuck with a slovenly looking oven. After a few years, nothing can be done to improve the oven's appearance.

This is no surprise to the manufacturers. They include cop outs in their manuals, like "soap, abrasive cleaners, or chemicals may permanently damage the continuous cleaning surface. Cooking spills may also cause permanent damage." So what good is an oven that you can neither clean, nor cook in? (Don't box my ears Sister. I know I should end a sentence with a preposition, but what's an aging French Canadian hockey player supposed to do when nothing else makes any sense, eh?)

- Self cleaning ovens, are the way to go if you want to spoil yourself a little. They are initially more expensive and are more costly to repair, but even a relatively cheap guy like me has one.

- The biggest cause for service calls on the self cleaning oven is being too rough on the latch handle during the cleaning cycle. Be gentle as a shy lover. Latch handles were made to lock and unlock rather easily. Never attempt to unlock an oven door latch before the cleaning cycle is complete. Impatience can easily cost you a $200 service call.

- Range / Microwave combinations look nice. They are a beautiful futuristic looking piece of equipment. However, if the microwave unit burns out, you will be forced to pay an extremely high repair bill. If you bought both appliances separately, you could just go out and buy a new microwave. Buying the appliances separately will save you a great deal of money.

- Indoor barbecues are a great feature if you like to wash grease from kitchen walls. They can also be responsible for some of the most mouth-wateringly tender, tempting chicken you have ever tasted. If you select this feature make certain that the ventilation system is installed very carefully.

- Touch pad controls. Look nice and futuristic don't they? Nothing like the old fashioned knobs on your mother's stove. In my opinion, the world is not ready for these things. They are very fragile, can not be repaired, and are horribly expensive to replace. Even industry studies note that the world may not be ready for touch pad controls."

- Overly sophisticated timing controls. Many people treat the timing units on ranges like inexpensive alarm clocks. They are not. If the unit goes wrong, you can easily be out a couple of hundred dollars replacement cost. As a general rule, the simpler the timing mechanism, the better.

Promise yourself that you will not buy a range that has a timing mechanism that you do not understand how to use before you leave the store. Make the salesperson explain the timer completely. Make him or her demonstrate. Make him or her teach you how to use it, and practice with the timer in the store. It is much better to make mistakes on the demonstrator model than on your brand new appliance.

1992 ELECTRIC RANGE SALES[1]	
Category	**Units Sold**
Built-In Ranges	**624,500**
Free Standing Ranges	**2,507,800**
Surface Cook tops	**441,700**
Total Units Sold:	**3,574,000**

[1]*Appliance Manufacturer*, March 1993, 22.

WHICH MAKES ARE MOST POPULAR?

1992 Electric Range Market Share[2]		
Make	**Ownership**	**Market Share**
G.E.	G.E.	30%
Whirlpool	Whirlpool	30%
Jenn-Air, Magic Chef & Hardwick	Maytag	17%
Frigidaire	Electrolux	15%
Caloric	Raytheon	7%

SHOPPING TIPS:

Compare repair and replacement costs. The three parts that have to be replaced most often on an electric range are the top burner, the oven element, and the timer.

If the appliance retailer at which you are shopping has a parts department, check out the retail costs of these parts. If the retailer does not have a parts & service department, go to a service company.

---

[2]*Appliance Manufacturer*, February 1993, 18.

If you want to really frighten yourself, compare the replacement costs of a hot wired burner and a plug in burner.

In the maintenance section of this chapter I have suggested ways that will give these components a long service life. It is up to you, the consumer, to find out what the after market prices are for these replacement parts. You will be amazed at how greatly the prices vary between the various companies. I have often heard consumers tell me that they would not have purchased a particular brand of electric range if they knew how expensively priced the replacement parts were. Please let this last sentence put caution in your shopping habits.

Part #1: The Top Burner

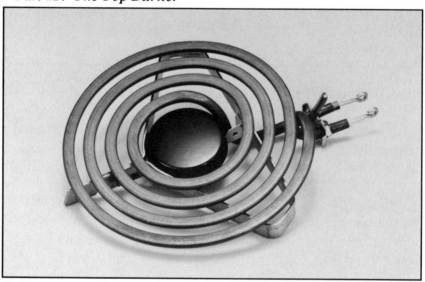

Top burners run from about $25.00 to $66.00 depending upon the range you buy. In 1993, a service call and labor required to replace this part varied from $45.00 to $95.00.

Part #2: The Oven Element

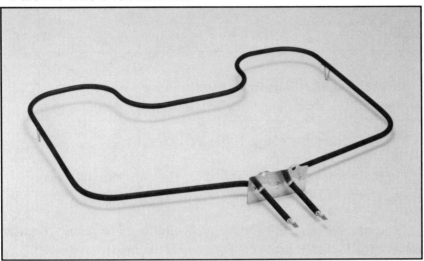

In 1993, oven element replacement costs varied from about $25.00 to $66.00 depending upon the range. A service call and labor will ranged from $45.00 to $95.00.

Part #3 The Timer

Hang on to your hats! In 1993, replacement costs for electric timers ranged from about $75.00 to $200.00 depending on the make. The service call and labor ranged between $70.00 and $125.00.

PART II: SETUP:

An electric range creates a great deal of heat. Keep it close to the sink and away from the Refrigerator. Here are some "musts."

Do make sure you have the stove plugged into a 250 watt power supply. Insufficient power is a prime cause of failure.

Do make sure the range is perfectly level.

Do make sure the cupboards over the range do not have heavy items in them. They can fall out and damage the range top.

Do make certain that the range is anchored in place so that it cannot tip forward and cause a serious accident.

Do make certain that a fire extinguisher is located close to the range. A stove top or oven fire can easily spread and cause a serious house fire or grave injury.

Do make certain that you pull the plug before you attempt do-it-yourself repairs.

PART III: USE:

Electric ranges are a lot like marriages. Treat them with respect and they last a lot longer. The old saw that familiarity breeds contempt is especially true with lovers and household appliances. The cooking top of an electric range is not a counter top. Don't use it as such. Don't put heavy pans and bowls full of whatever on the cooking surface just to get them out of the way. Above all, **never** slam anything on the burner. Slamming the burner is a great deal like hitting an electric socket with a sledge hammer. Sooner or later you are going to break something.

While we're talking about slamming, **don't slam the oven door.** This is certainly a case where a lot of people do not know their own strength. A slammed oven door can spring the door and throw the thermostat out of whack. Make sure that you do not use the open oven door like a shelf. Oven doors were not meant to support heavy roasts. Using the door for a shelf can spring the door and cause an expensive service call.

REMEMBER: CHILDREN ARE CURIOUS.

They will pull on the handles of pans just to see what is inside. Cooking should be done on the rear burners. Cooking or boiling water on front burners is an invitation to disaster. According to the Delta Faucet Company, every year 37,000 children 14 years of age and younger are treated for burns by hot liquids, hot food and hot tap water. Many die or suffer disfigurement. Most scalds happen in the kitchen. **Please keep your children safe. If you have children, cook on rear burners only.**

PART IV: MAINTENANCE:

General:

1. Make a rule to clean up spills as soon as they occur. The longer a spill remains, the more difficult it becomes to remove. A good organic cleaner, such as Simple Green™, and water is recommended. Never use as abrasive cleaner.

2. Burned or heavily stained areas on the burner or reflective surfaces under the burners may be cleaned with Bon Ami™. Use the bar, not the powder.

CAUTION: REMEMBER YOUR STOVE IS CHARGED WITH 220 VOLTS OF ELECTRICITY. THAT IS MORE THAN ENOUGH TO KILL YOU. PULL THE BIG PLUG IN THE BACK FROM THE POWER SUPPLY BEFORE YOU ATTEMPT TO CLEAN AROUND THE BURNERS OR OTHER HEATING ELEMENTS OR DO ANY REPAIR WORK.

(WAR STORY) When I was a kid in Canada, my dad used to take us kids out to the beach. In the afternoon he'd have us dig a hole in the sand. Then, we'd build a fire in the hole and keep feeding it logs. The sand around the fire would get so hot it would actually start boiling.

When my dad judged that he had enough coals, he would put this great big cast iron Dutch Oven filled with navy pea beans, pieces of chicken, water, spices and I don't know what all, in the coals, and we would fill the hole and cover the coals and pot with sand. Then, we would start another fire on the sand above the pot. After a few hours we would let the fire die down, unearth the pot and treat ourselves to one of the most delectable meals I have ever tasted.

This is not just a story for nostalgia buffs. Believe it or not, my dad was using the same heat transference technology on the beach, all those many years ago, that you use when you heat something on the burners or in the oven of the most advanced electric stove.

Inside the electric burner or in the oven heating element is a small electrical wire which is encased in sand. The wire heats the sand and causes it to boil. The boiling sand heats the outer casing red hot, and you cook on it.

You may well ask yourself what has this to do with daily maintenance of my stove. OK, I'll ask it, What the heck does this have to do with the daily maintenance of my stove?

Well, one of the most common occurrences of cooking, either frying, broiling or baking, is that something boils over. Quite often, that something, like the tomato sauce for spaghetti, or even a delicious deep dish apple pie, if you're baking, contains acid.

If you are sloppy about cleaning up those spills, little by little, the acid will eat away the outer metal sheath. One day, the pitting will get too bad and Bang! a hole in the burner will explode and a piece of hot molten metal will shoot across the room.

If you are lucky, you will only be frightened out of a year's growth. If you are unlucky, someone will be standing in front of that red hot piece of shrapnel and a serious injury may have occurred. So a word to the wise, take care of those spills and drips, before they turn your electric stove into a lethal weapon.

3. Burner pans are made to reflect heat upward. Any stain decreases the efficiency of your burner.

When something boils over the pan should be cleaned as soon as the burner is cool enough to allow you to remove the burner pan. To clean, use water and an organic cleaner like Simple Green™. If that doesn't work, try soaking the pan and try again. If the stains are still "hanging tough", use a bar of Bon Ami™. Never use an abrasive, like scouring powder or a scouring pad.

If the burner pans get so stained that they no longer look good or reflect properly, buy genuine replacement burner pans from your appliance store or service department. The cheap, universal replacement pans you can get at hardware stores are too light to hold their brightness for long.

Never use aluminum foil to act as a reflective surface on top of an old burner pan. The foil is too light to work adequately, will become loose and can cause a very nasty electric short.

PART IV: TROUBLE SHOOTING

Most range manufacturers publish repair manuals for their appliances. It is a very good idea to look at the repair manual for the appliance, while you are shopping for the appliance. The repair manual should be very clear, with lots of photos. The repairs should look easy. The easier the repairs are, the more consumer driven the manufacturer is. Buy the repair manual at the same time you buy the appliance.

WARNING: Do not take chances with your life. After you have decided what the problem is, pull the main power plug before you attempt to make repairs.

PROBLEM: The range is turned on, but nothing is happening.

Look in the back and make certain that the power supply is plugged in. If it is, try the fuse box in the basement. If that's on, look for the fuses in the stove, and take them to be tested at your local, full service hardware store. Replace if necessary.

PROBLEM: Burner doesn't heat.

Try another burner and see if you have a power problem to the entire stove top, or the problem is isolated to an individual burner. If nothing on top works, look in the back and make sure the stove is plugged in, then turn the oven on and make sure you have heat in the oven. If you have heat in the oven but not the stove top, it may be a fuse problem.

Some manufacturers install fuses in their ranges. They look like an ordinary 15 amp fuse in your circuit box, but are often very hard to find. If you look hard and cannot find a fuse, call the manufacturer, tell them the model number of your range and ask where the fuse is located.

If the problem is isolated to a single burner, you will have to replace that burner. Pull out elements are easy. Just pull it out, go to your parts supplier and get a replacement. Then, plug it in. There is also the possibility that the ceramic fixture the element plugs into has been cracked (usually by someone putting a very heavy weight on the element when the element, itself, was improperly inserted into the fixture). Ceramic fixtures are easy to replace. You can buy them at your parts supplier. Complete instructions come with the fixture.

Hot wired elements should usually be replaced by a service person.

PROBLEM: Oven element does not work.

Oven elements are very easy to replace. Open the oven door and look at the back of the oven. You will see that the element is held in place by two screws. Remove the screws and gently pull the element out about four inches. Disconnect the two wires connected to the element and remove the element from the oven.

Inspect the element to see if there is a hole in it. If not, you can check to see if the element is any good by hooking up a 110 volt test cord to both ends of the element. If the element is an good, it will get warm, but not red hot after a few minutes. Another way to test the element is to take it to your local hardware store and ask them to check it with an Ohmmeter.

If the element is defective, take it to a parts supplier and get a replacement element. If the element is good reconnect it and recheck to see if the oven heats. If it still doesn't, it's time to call in a service person.

PROBLEM: Oven light won't go on.

Simple. There is a 40 Watt bulb made specifically for the high heat temperatures in the oven. Most hardware stores, and all appliance service departments, should have it.

To replace, remove the cover being very careful not to damage the seal that fits behind the cover. Pull out the bulb and replace. Then carefully reattach the cover.

PROBLEM: Door springs are sprung and the door is no longer sealing properly, allowing heat to escape.

Oven door springs are very important because they are responsible for the door staying open when in the downward position as well as for sealing in the heat when the door is closed. The springs are attached to a hinge underneath the door.

To readjust the door hinges, you usually just have to remove the bottom storage drawer. The hinge will then be plainly visible and easy to adjust.

Some ovens have their hinges located inside the door itself. In these cases the entire door has to be taken apart to get at the hinge. Consult your owner's manual.

Chapter 8

GAS RANGES

PART I: SHOPPING?

FIVE QUICK QUESTIONS TO ASK:

1. Can I purchase the old style pilot type range?

2. How long is the warranty on the igniter?

3. How do I obtain service when and if I need it?

4. Do you have any cooking classes offered for consumers?

5. Do you have a demonstrator model hooked up so that I can check the flame adjustment?

FIVE QUALITY FEATURES TO LOOK FOR:

1. Burner controls located so that small fry will find it hard to reach them.

2. Burner grates which are heavier than others.

3. Top and grates lift up for easy cleaning.

4. A superior warranty.

5. A convenient storage drawer.

THINGS TO THINK ABOUT

The decision whether to buy a gas or electric range is up to the cook. The case in favor of gas is that gas cooking is about one third the price of electric cooking. Gas burners give instant heat and good cooks tell me they can fine tune gas stove top heat level to a far greater degree than with an electric range.

It's not all one sided however. Electric range top cooking is far cleaner than gas. Gas burner flame marks the bottoms of pots and pans. Over the years you will find that gas yellows and adds a tacky residue to walls, ceilings and appliances.

Some other drawbacks of gas ranges include discoloration of the range top surface with age and usage; knobs have a tendency to break and discolor easily; and the burner grates turn brown with usage.

If the decision is to buy a gas range, you will find that there are two different types on the market. The old fashioned standing pilot kind and the newer ignitor" models. The old kind burns constantly, burning your money along with the gas. The ignitor models conserve energy, but you will spend your savings times a factor of ten when you have to replace the oven ignitor.

If you bake or broil a great deal, the new machines can wind up costing you a great deal of money (my viewpoint is not one which will bring many manufacturers begging for my endorsement.).

You no doubt remember your mother's or your grandmother's gas stove. That thing cooked its heart out and nothing ever went wrong with it. Oh, after about twenty or thirty years, the oven thermostat was out of kilter, but ma just turned up the thermostat and that was all taken care of.

Well, times change. Indestructible gas ranges do not make the owners of appliance stores or service managers very happy. Nor do nonexistent replacement part sales make manufacturers very much money. Remember "Caveat Emptor", the rule of the market place, "let the buyer beware."

You always have the final responsibility to make an intelligent purchase. Let me suggest that you be very particular in assuring yourself of the quality of the oven igniter on the gas range you buy. Make certain that it is guaranteed and that the store, as well as the manufacturer is standing behind that guarantee.

Some models of Magic Chef gas ranges use a spark type igniter instead of a glow type. My experience with this spark type igniter has been very good. It lasts longer and costs a lot less to replace than the glow type. I can not understand why many other manufacturers have not designed spark type igniters into their equipment.

In the early 1980's the government pressured the gas appliance manufacturers into designing reduced energy costs into new models. This arm twisting by the government cost the appliance manufacturers millions of dollars in design and engineering costs. One way to get all that development money back, plus interest, would have been to design a very short lived oven igniter into the equipment.

I do not know if that is what happened. I do know that almost all the oven igniters I have seen are very low quality, fragile, and expensive to replace. Some are so cheaply made that they can be broken by simply shutting the door too hard.

A few years back one manufacturer used sub standard metal in the burner tubes of their gas stoves. I do not know if this was a bad batch of metal, or if the standard had been lowered. I do know, that as a service man I found that the tubes were so bad they fell apart soon after hookup, permitting open flame to burn directly into the igniter. To my knowledge the defective ranges were never recalled, or had the defective parts replaced. The manufacturer just kept selling replacement igniters.

Before you buy, make sure you consult a good current consumer rating magazine that tests each years models thoroughly. Determine which brands and which specific models they recommend most highly, then make your selection from the best. This is not the time to scrimp. If a low rated model costs a hundred bucks less when you buy it, I can assure you that when you factor in the extra service calls you will need over a ten year period, the low rated stove will turn out to be the most expensive in the store.

Here's a chart that shows who the sales volume leaders are. Keep in mind, Chevrolet sells a lot more cars than BMW; but a lot of doctors and lawyers I know, tell me BMW makes a pretty good car.

WHICH MAKES ARE MOST POPULAR?

1992 Gas Range Market Share[1]		
Make	**Ownership**	**Market Share**
Jenn-Air, Hardwick, Magic Chef	Maytag	27%
Frigidaire, Tappan	Electrolux	25%
Caloric Roper	Raytheon	22%

ALSO COMPARE REPLACEMENT COSTS BEFORE YOU BUY.

There is a wide difference in the prices charged for replacement parts by the various manufacturers. Some will charge 50% or more for an almost identical part than other manufactures. I have been told that this difference may not be greed, but may be caused by the way the accounting department is allocating charges for parts storage, etc.

To my mind, it does not matter if it is greed or merely book-keeping stupidity. I don't like being over charged for parts. If you feel the same way, compare repair and replacement costs before you buy.

---

[1]*Appliance Manufacturer,* February 1993, 18.

The three parts that have to be replaced most often on an gas range are:

1. Oven Igniter

2. Oven Safety Valve

3. Thermostat

If the appliance retailer at which you are shopping has a parts & service department, check out the retail costs of these parts and what the service charges would be to replace them. If the retailer does not have a parts & service department, go to a service company.

Part #1: The Oven Igniter

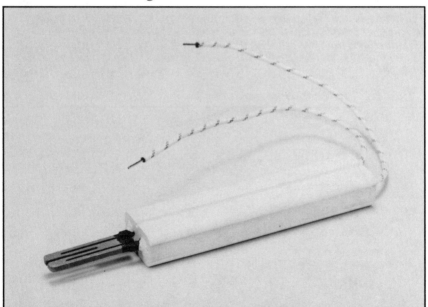

The oven igniter is the little part that actually ignites the gas when you turn on the oven. Depending on the manufacturer, in 1993 this part had a replacement cost of between $30.00 and $90.00. The service call and labor would usually range from $60.00 to $100.00.

Part #2: The Oven Safety Valve

The safety valve is a very important piece of equipment. This little part has a mind of its own. When you turn the thermostat on your oven "on", it will not allow the gas to be released if it senses that the igniter, or glow bar, is not functioning properly and there would be faulty ignition. Depending on the manufacturer, the 1993 retail replacement costs of this part was between $55.00 and $95.00. The service call and labor would add between $60.00 and $100.00.

Part #3 The Oven Thermostat

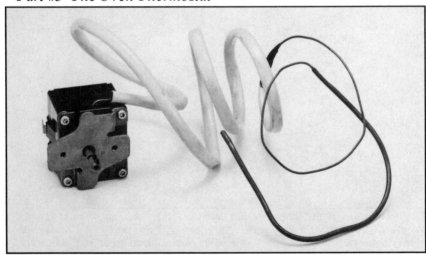

The thermostat lets you control how hot it gets in the oven. 1993 retail replacement costs vary between $60.00 and $150.00. The service and labor will add another $60.00 to $100.00.

Parts costs are very important to the Do-It-Yourselfer. For those of you who do not have the time to do the job yourself, it is very important to compare both the actual parts and the service charges for these items.

Don't trust my figures. They may be outdated or not apply in your part of the country. Get the parts, time and labor costs for these items from your appliance retailer before you buy. Then, let your fingers do the walking, and check out the same costs at local independent service contractors. Add an extra hour for diagnostic service to the proposed charges.

Just a little aside. You now know more about gas ranges than many appliance sales people and we're only half way through the chapter. Wouldn't it be nice if you could be confident that you could walk into an appliance store and get this kind of information without even asking? It's time for you consumers to demand more informative presentations from thoroughly trained, knowledgeable sales people.

PART II: SETUP:

Safety is especially important in the kitchen. A gas range is an excellent, but potentially lethal appliance. The kitchen is the heart of the home. Every year, over 100,000 fires are reported to be started by cooking equipment, so take a little extra time, money and effort to make your kitchen safe. Here are some "musts."

Do install two gas shutoffs. When installing a gas range, have the installer put in two shut off valves on the gas line. One in the basement on the black iron pipe. The other should go on the flexible line directly behind the range. That way, if a fire starts, you can shut off all burners immediately. Turn off the line behind the range first, then go downstairs and also turn off the gas at the black pipe source.

Do make sure that there are no highly flammable objects hanging from cupboards or walls directly above the burners.

Do install both a smoke detector and a fire extinguisher. Remember, when you have a gas range you are literally "playing with fire." Every kitchen should have a smoke detector and a fire extinguisher. When you have gas, a high priced detector that also detects carbon monoxide and leaking gas is a good idea. There are many cheap detectors on the market. Your family is too important to buy the cheap stuff. Field tests have shown that up to 40% of some brands are ineffective. (Some bargain!)

PART III: USE:

The following paragraphs may make me sound like a busy body, or a maiden aunt. I'm sorry folks, I've read the literature, I've spoken to the firemen and 911 operators, I've toured the burn wards. I know these things can happen and I don't want them to happen to anyone in your house.

All stoves are dangerous. Especially to very young children. If there are young ones in the house, do most of your cooking on the back burners. Pots filled with boiling liquid (water, soup, spaghetti sauce, etc.) are especially dangerous. The handles are irresistible to small fry. When their curiosity causes them to pull down on the handle of a pan of hot water, the scalding they receive will give them (and you) a lifetime of pain and anguish.

Number two on my hit list is using the open, oven door as a counter top. A couple of heavy pans on that door, can not only ruin the springs (that just costs you money), it also makes the stove out of balance. If junior sits on the door, or starts playing around with the pots, the entire range may tip forward and spill whatever is on the stove on the guilty party.

PART IV: MAINTENANCE:

Many of the problems which occur on gas ranges can be directly attributable to dirt. Grease and food spills can cause plugged and misaligned burner flames. So clean up spills immediately.

DAILY:

1. Clean range top with a 10 to 1 solution of water and an organic cleaner like Simple Green®, Breeze® or Clear Magic®.

EVERY SIX MONTHS:

1. Remove all the parts from the top of the stove and wash them in a soap and very hot water solution. Let them soak a little while. Clean out the holes on the burners with a pin. Rinse and dry thoroughly.

TROUBLE SHOOTING:

OLD FASHIONED PILOT LIGHT MODELS:

PROBLEM: Burner on pilot light type gas range does not light when knob is turned.

You can stop lighting the burner with a match if you keep the burner tubes clean and clear. The problem is usually just that the aluminum tube which allows the pilot to ignite the gas coming from the burner has become plugged. If you follow the aluminum tube to the face of the burner pot you will see three or four small holes. Bend a safety or straight pin and push it in the holes to clear away the dirt that is blocking the holes. When you clear the blockage, the problem should be solved.

PROBLEM: The grate on my stove is old and rusty looking.

Gas stove grates take quite a beating from the open flame. If they really start looking bad you can sand off the oxidation and repaint them with a special stove paint you can get at any good hardware store.

PROBLEM: The pilot takes a long time to ignite the burner and when it finally does, there is a mini-explosion.

This is usually proof of a clogged pilot tube. Clean the holes as I described above. It should solve the problem.

PROBLEM: The pilot flame is too big.

Pilot flames can be adjusted. Follow the tube to the source and you will find a small set screw which you can adjust for pilot size. The smaller the pilot flame, the less gas you will consume. The flame should be just large enough to ignite the burner within three seconds.

PROBLEM: Oven door bangs open when the oven burner is ignited.

The door flies open when a mini explosion occurs due to gas build up caused by delayed ignition. This is almost always a sure sign of a dirty ignition tube. The burner tube through which the flame flows from the pilot has been plugged. You will find that this tube has a little end piece with a hole in it. This piece can be removed and cleaned.

You will notice that the burner tube also has a slit in it which goes from one side of the tube to the other. This slit allows the gas to burn on both sides of the burner tube. You can clean this slit with a razor blade, allowing the gas to escape and burn evenly.

PROBLEM: The tube is clean and the oven burner still is not igniting properly.

If the oven still is not igniting properly, you may have to replace the oven safety valve. This is one of the most common failures on a gas stove.

The oven safety valve is mounted inside and against the back wall in your oven. The oven safety valve contains an orifice which feeds gas to the burner tube. The burner tube leads to it and joins into it.

Mercury Operating Valve Models

The first thing to do is to check to see if there are any electric wires attached to the safety valve. If there are no wires, you have a mercury operating valve. You will see that it contains a small tube leading from it to the pilot flame.

Make certain that tube has not fallen out of its holder, and that the pilot flame engulfs the end of the tube when the pilot is turned on. If you see that the tube has fallen out of its holder, you should be able to put it back into position with no problem.

To check to see if the safety valve is the problem, you will need a propane type cigarette lighter. Turn the oven thermostat up to 300° F. You will notice the pilot flame becomes larger. This additional flame and heat should expand the mercury in the small tube and open the safety valve allowing gas to flow into the burner tube.

If it doesn't, add the flame of your cigarette lighter to the existing pilot flame. This additional flame and heat should expand the mercury in the small tube and open the safety valve allowing gas to flow into burner. If the burner ignites, change the oven safety valve.

After you have removed the safety valve, tap the open end in the palm of your hand to make the mercury beads show themselves. If you can see the beads, it is another sign the safety valve has to be replaced.

You can pick up the safety valve in the parts department of your favorite appliance store.

Replacing the safety valve is simple.

1. Shut off the gas supply to the range.

2. Remove the fitting from the end of the valve.

3. Look for three screws. Two hold the valve in place, and one small screw holds the mercury tube in its holder. Carefully unscrew the screws and lift out the old safety valve and replace it with the new.

4. Use care when positioning the new safety valve, that you do not break the end of the small capillary tube when placing it into its holder. Make sure that it is fitted properly, so that the pilot flame engulfs it.

Don't just throw the old safety valve into the garbage. Mercury is a very hazardous contaminant and will harm the environment. Call city hall and find out where it should be taken for proper disposal.

Electrically Fired Models

The flame safety switch is another method used for oven ignition in the old style pilot gas oven. This system has an oven safety valve with two electrical leads on top of the valve. (Home Handyman Alert:) Put down your trusty 110 volt tester, you could ruin this delicate mechanism. This electrically operated system uses millivolts of electricity, activated by the enlarged secondary pilot when the oven thermostat is set to the desired temperature.

This system also has a small tube leading into the pilot flame as a backup. To check to see if the safety valve needs to be replaced, simply detach the two wires from the bottom of the safety valve and put them together. If your oven ignites, the safety switch is defective and should be replaced.

NEW STYLE IGNITER MODELS:

PROBLEM: The igniter keeps sparking, even when the burners are turned off.

Top burner igniters are usually the snap type. They can be very sensitive to humidity or stove top spillage. When this occurs, try heating the area behind the knobs with a hair dryer. These top burner igniters are real work horses and should last the life of your stove. Improper ignition usually means dirt. Clean thoroughly and the problem should be resolved. If not, read the paragraph on Igniter Control Module replacement at the end of the oven problems section.

PROBLEM: The oven doesn't go on when it is turned on and the thermostat set.

The oven igniter is mounted to the burner tube inside the oven and can easily be replaced by the Do-It-Yourselfer. The electrical oven igniter has two wires leading to it and two screws which hold it to the mounting. Since this is one of the most temperamental parts of many gas ranges, you can save a lot of money by doing it yourself.

In operation, when you turn up the oven thermostat, the electrical current flows through the igniter and it glows red hot. After the igniter glows red, it sends millivolts of electricity to the oven safety valve, opening the valve and allowing the gas to enter and burst into flame when it hits the red hot igniter.

That's the theory, anyway. In practice, the igniter can glow red hot, yet not shed enough millivolts of electricity to open the all important gas valve. If the valve doesn't open, the gas does not ignite.

The solution usually is just replacing the igniter. When you get the replacement part, try to find a place that will let you return the new igniter if you install it and it still does not work.

PROBLEM: The igniter is not getting red hot.

The problem is usually a blown fuse. The igniter fuse is mounted in a small holder similar to a car radio holder. Unfortunately, every manufacturer seems to delight in hiding the igniter fuse in a different location. You'll have to hunt for it. If you can't find it, call the manufacturer's toll free telephone number and ask where they hid the fuse.

PROBLEM: Help, I'm still not getting ignition.

If all else fails, you may have to replace the control module that sends the power to the igniters in both the oven and the range surface. This is the last part to check because it almost never goes bad. (OK, let's be honest. One of the reasons I don't check it right away is because I usually have a devil of a time finding it.) Electrical design teams take a fiendish joy is hiding gas stove control modules so well that no one, not even their own service departments, can find them.

If you decide it must be the control module, it is often behind the back panel of the appliance. Before you replace it, take it into the service department and have it checked to see if it is defective.

The control module is a plastic box with a bunch of terminals to which the igniter lead wires are attached. Disconnect the wires and you can easily replace the module.

PROBLEM: The oven is too hot (cold). I want to adjust the setting.

The temperature adjustment of your oven is sometimes located behind the thermostat knob. Take off the thermostat knob and look for a small screw with a plus and minus sign, or notches. Take a screwdriver and carefully adjust the screw up or down.

Be careful. This is also a favorite place for the manufacturers to locate the LP or natural gas switch. If you see the initials LP and N, do not touch the set screw. Accidentally switching from natural gas to LP gas operation could cause an explosion that would destroy your house and everyone in it.

On that pleasant note I will bring this chapter to a close.

Chapter 9

MICROWAVE OVENS

PART I: SHOPPING?

FIVE QUICK QUESTIONS TO ASK:

1. **Which has the best warranty?**

2. **Where does the microwave vent, through the front or the back?** Front is better. It can't be blocked so easily.

3. **What is the wattage output?** The higher the wattage, the faster the microwave works.

4. **Are there cooking classes available?** You need them if you are not an expert.

5. **Where is the fuse?** -Trust me, this is a harder question than you think.

FIVE QUALITY FEATURES TO LOOK FOR:

1. Fast clean surfaces outside and inside.

2. A defrost cycle.

3. An oven that is big enough for your needs.

4. A sturdy door that opens conveniently.

5. No touch pad controls.

THINGS TO THINK ABOUT.

I read a consumer magazine article once that described the microwave oven as the greatest discovery since fire. I agree. Today, the country is filled with millions of people, singles, working mothers, senior citizens, and me, who wouldn't get a hot meal without their trusty microwave.

The microwave oven was discovered by accident by a Dr. Spencer. At least I think that was his name. He was standing in front of the path of radar waves and a chocolate bar he had in his pants pocket melted.

He and his colleagues tinkered around and came up with the first microwave oven which weighed several hundred pounds.

During the Second World War it was very hush, hush, but microwave ovens were used in the transport planes flying our military over seas. After the war the microwave oven was gradually introduced to the public and revolutionized the market place.

Today's microwaves are much lighter and faster and far less expensive. They save time and energy. And folks, let me tell you, you haven't seen anything yet. You can expect the microwaves of the near future to be voice activated and even take orders over the phone. By the time this unique piece of equipment is fully developed it may have replaced every other method of cooking in the average home.

All that good stuff agreed to, be advised, the microwave is also potentially the most dangerous piece of equipment in your kitchen. Microwaves are not like radio waves that harmlessly pass through walls and into your living room stereo with no ill effect to anyone. Microwaves can zap you. They must be kept inside the oven cavity or the family is in danger.

That said, let me reassure you. I spent three years testing microwaves for a major manufacturer. In all those three years, testing thousands of appliances, using the most sophisticated testing equipment available, I did not run across one microwave oven that leaked rays.

To this date, I have never encountered a microwave oven that permitted dangerous amounts of microwaves to escape. They are my favorite cooking appliance (There are some people who maintain that I have had one too many hockey sticks to the head when I say that).

Microwaves are created by the magnetron tube inside the oven. The microwaves are kept inside the oven cavity by metal shielding and a specially designed door. The door latch mechanism is made so that whenever the microwave oven door is opened, the power to the magnetron tube is automatically turned off. This door is your first line of defense, and your most likely cause of failure. If you spring the door and destroy the seal, microwaves could leak from the unit.

Thoroughly confused? Good. Lets go shopping.

SHOPPING TIPS?

Buy a microwave oven like you would buy a computer. Get what's best for your needs, but realize that state of the art today, will be old news tomorrow.

Do your homework with *Consumer Reports*, then get the same machine, or at least the same features that they recommend. However, there are so many machines out there, look for the features you need and see which appliance gives you the best deal on features.

Here are a few drawbacks to some of the most popular features:

- Touch pad controls are very expensive to repair. Sometimes more than the cost of the product.

- Inside turntables save you the task of turning the food by hand, but can also be very expensive to repair.

- Removable glass trays are easy to clean, but expensive if you break them during cleaning.

1992 MICROWAVE OVEN SALES

In 1992 there were a total of 7,967,000 microwave ovens sold in the United States. The only trouble with this figure is that in 1990, 9,626,000 microwaves were sold. In 1988, the number was 10,988,000.

You don't have to be a Wall Street analyst to see that the numbers are going in the wrong direction. Apparently almost everyone who wants a microwave oven, already has one. Microwaves have been in the market for twenty years now. It may be that all that is left is the replacement market.

WHICH MAKES ARE MOST POPULAR?

1992 Microwave Oven Market Share[1]	
Make	**Market Share**
Sharp	20%
Samsung	18%
Matsushita Incl. Panasonic & Quasar	17%
Electrolux Frigidaire	10%
Goldstar	10%
Sanyo Fisher	7%
Matag Magic Chef	6%

Energy Efficiency.

Not all microwave ovens are created equal. Although a professional unit may not look much different than something you can pick up for $175.00, there is a big difference in the machines.

The way to compare microwave ovens is to compare **Size VS Wattage VS Speed VS Price.** When comparing ovens, you first have to determine whether the oven is big enough to suit your needs. Trying to cook a whole chicken in an oven that will only hold a cup of soup won't work.

---

[1] *Appliance Manufacturer*, February 1993, 18.

The next two criteria go together. The higher the Wattage, the faster the cooking speed. You will be surprised at how much difference there is in microwave ovens when you look into these criteria.

Finally, you have to be able to afford to take it out of the store.

Don't go for cheap. Cheap usually means small, poorly constructed, low powered. None of which will make you smile if you are trying to make the family bacon and poached eggs in the morning.

Parts & Replacement Costs

Now, compare parts and replacement costs. The three parts that have to be replaced most often on a Microwave Oven are: Fuses, Touch Pads and Magnetron Tubes.

Check out the retail costs of these parts and the service charges at your retailer. Double check him with at least one independent. After you've double checked the prices, you will probably agree with me that, unless you have a top of the line unit, it usually doesn't pay to have an extensive repair on a microwave oven.

Microwave ovens are a great deal like computers. The field is progressing so fast, that by the time you have to repair your old microwave oven, you will probably want a new one.

PART II: SETUP:

The microwave oven is a very easy appliance to set up. You just have to make certain that it is on a flat surface and is installed with enough air space around it for proper ventilation.

An unimpeded flow of cool air coming into the microwave oven is important to keep the magnetron tube as cool as possible. Overheated air can cause premature failure. Proper venting of air exhausted from the oven is just as important.

Be especially careful with models that vent out the back. If you install a back venting model flush to the wall you will burn out the equipment in no time and technically the Warranty should be void because you will have destroyed the equipment.

A good power supply is the next most important factor. It is essential that the microwave oven have its own electric circuit. Be sure to install a surge protector. Power spikes can destroy your new microwave.

PART III: USE:

1. Be careful not to stack things around the microwave oven that will cut off the air flow. Remember, plenty of "breathing space" around the front, back, sides and top of the appliance is essential Hot air can cause premature failure of the magnetron tube, ruining the appliance. Unrestricted air intake and out flow are equally important.

2. It is common for a microwave oven to have hot spots. To determine where these spots are in your machine, put four small containers filled with the exact same amount of water in the four corners of the oven cavity. Set the microwave to run a minute and one half on high.

For this next step be careful that the water is not so hot that you burn yourself. When the time has elapsed, carefully test the water temperature in each of the four corners with a different finger. Cold water is the sign of a cold spot. There is no way I know to even out the heat capability of a microwave oven. Just remember where the cold spot is and place the food accordingly.

3. Clear away everything in the oven after each use. Certain food products, such as popcorn, or snacks, can cause a fire inside the oven cavity. Always consult the owner's manual before trying to prepare a recipe with which you are not familiar.

4. Never slam a microwave oven door. I have seen too many latch mechanisms broken by the slamming of the door. Close microwave oven doors gently and the latch mechanism will last forever.

5. The touch pad controls on most microwave ovens are very sensitive and extremely expensive to replace. Be gentle.

6. As previously mentioned the microwave should have its own electric circuit. Use a surge protector on the power line. Power surges and sudden fall-offs can ruin the oven.

Never use a microwave oven when your community's public utility has declared a "brown out" and reduced the power supply. The reduced rate of power can ruin your microwave.

7. Play it safe. Do not make a habit of staring at the food through the glass panel on the door while the food is being cooked. Your eyes are especially vulnerable. While it is true that Microwave emissions dissipate at a distance of 12 to 18 inches (in other words they are gone and can't cause any damage.) and the chance that your microwave oven will ever leak microwaves is far less than your chance of winning a State Lottery. Don't take a chance. Your eyes are too important.

8. Cooking lessons are vital if you are going to get maximum use out of your microwave. If you are going to invest good money, learn how to use the equipment properly. Just because you have cooked successfully for twenty years does not mean you know beans about microwave cooking.

If you don't believe me, just try poaching an egg. I want it soft and runny on the inside, firm white on the outside, and I definitely do not want it blown to smithereens and spread all over the six walls of the microwave.

Most people who read this paragraph could not poach that egg. Poaching eggs is simple. Much of what people say about microwave ovens effecting the taste of foods adversely is caused by the person doing the cooking not knowing how to use the equipment. Used properly, microwave ovens should enhance the taste of foods, especially vegetables.

Pay strict attention to "standing times" when cooking in a microwave oven. Remember that with a microwave the food molecules are moving around much faster than in conventional cooking. That means that when you take the food out of the microwave and set it on the counter, the food is still cooking.

If you do not wait for the proper standing time, the food may seem to be undone and you will be tempted to put the food back in the "mike" and give it a couple of extra minutes. This generosity on your part can easily cause the food to be overdone.

PART IV: MAINTENANCE:

Daily:

Daily cleaning of the inside of a microwave oven can be made easier if you heat water to boiling. The steam will make it easier to get small, baked-on particles off the sides of the microwave.

Never use a rough surface, such as steel wool or the rough side of a dish washing sponge to clean the shiny metal floor and sides of a microwave oven. The shiny metal sides are specially made to reflect the micro waves. Rough materials will scratch the shiny surface and reduce their reflective ability.

The door seal should be kept clean of dirt and food particles. The bottom section of an oven door that opens top to bottom is especially vulnerable to collecting deposits of gunk. If you let these build up, you can cause the door not to seal properly and escaping emissions could burn you or someone else in the room.

Always use extreme caution while the microwave is running. Microwave emissions can burn a person just like an open flame, only faster.

Every 6 Months:

Remove the plastic ceiling shield (if removable), and give the plastic a good wash with soap and water. Dry carefully and replace immediately. **Do not touch the tube. Do not run the microwave oven without the guard.**

Check around the back and sides of the oven to make certain that articles are not collecting that could decrease the air flow to the microwave oven.

PART V: TROUBLE SHOOTING

PROBLEM: I've cleaned the microwave several times and can't get rid of an odor.

Odors which won't leave after a normal cleaning can usually be removed with one of two tricks.

1. Boil a half cup of lemon juice mixed with a cup of water for five minutes.

2. Boil 2 cups of tomato juice in the oven. Then, let it stand for a couple of hours.

In a previous chapter, I stressed the importance of unplugging the power at its source whenever you have to make repairs. In the case of a microwave oven, I want to not only stress, but scare the pants off you.

Not too long ago I interviewed a man on my radio show who had spent ten years repairing microwave ovens. He worked in a store that also sold parts. He was a thorough professional.

One day, while working on, and testing, a microwave oven, he had to leave it to take care of a parts customer. When finished with the customer he went back to work on the oven. He observed what looked like a loose wire. Without remembering that the appliance was plugged in, he grabbed the wire with his fingers.

He was thrown to the floor and stopped breathing. Luckily, the customer who had just purchased some parts from him had not left the counter yet, and was a registered nurse. She saw that he had been electrocuted and rushed to his aid giving him mouth to mouth resuscitation.

The man owes his life to the quick action of his customer. He was in the hospital in a coma for three weeks, and on a lung machine for six months.

The good news is that he is still alive. The sad news is that he will never be completely cured.

If you ever decide to try to fix your microwave oven, pull the darn plug. Do I make myself clear?

Even when the unit is unplugged, there is a capacitor inside which is charged with voltage. If you touch it, you can burn a small hole in the end of your finger. The voltage may travel from one hand and out through the other. If this happens it will rack your shoulder back and cause an excruciating pain that you will remember until the day you die.

Still not afraid? Well try this on for size. The voltage in a microwave oven is so great that, if it shocks you, it grabs you. In other words, you can't pull your hand away. It will keep sizzling current through your body until your feet burn through the shoes you are wearing.

I am now going to tell you a few things that you may want to try if you have trouble with your microwave oven. I am going to tell you how to do very few things because I don't want your life on my hands.

If you try the things I am going to tell you and your microwave oven still does not work properly you will have to consider bringing it in for service or throwing it away and getting a new one.

Remember what I said about microwave ovens improving all the time? An average service call on a difficult problem (in the next two pages I will have told you how to fix all the easy problems) is going to cost you between $150 and $ 300. If your microwave oven is not still under warranty it may pay you to throw your problem away and get a new microwave oven.

PROBLEM: My microwave oven does not work.

Check to see if your appliance is plugged in to the outlet. If it is, run over to the fuse box and make certain a fuse isn't blown, or the circuit breaker hasn't stopped the power. If those two things are all right, you have probably blown a fuse inside your microwave oven.

The first thing you do before attempting anything else is (I've told you at least three times already) remove the electrical plug from the outlet. You can read the rest of these instructions, but don't try to do anything to the microwave oven until the electrical charge has completely dissipated. This can take a good deal of time. I describe how to check that the appliance has discharged about two paragraphs down. Don't take short cuts.

Fuse replacement is the only thing I'm going to suggest you do. Don't feel abused. I'm saving you a hundred dollars easy with just this one tip. Service people love to play games with consumers over fuse replacement. Doing it yourself can save a great deal of money.

In most cases the fuse looks like an old fashioned car fuse. It is usually located in a holder on the right side and can be removed with the small end of a screwdriver. A little pressure and it just pops out.

Other kinds of microwave fuses look like a common round household fuse or a smaller version of a cartridge fuse.

Here's a picture of the three types of microwave fuses. Ninety percent of them look like the white cylinder at the bottom.

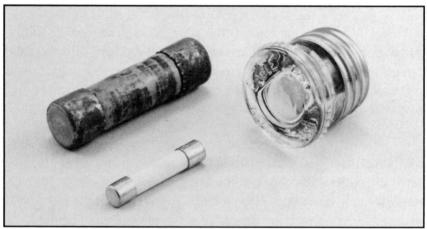

Three types of microwave fuses.

Now that I've told you what to look for, let me tell you when to look for it. You look for the fuse after the plug has been pulled; after the microwave has proven incapable of any sound, any light, any light in the key pad. In other words, you monkey around with the appliance only after you can be reasonable certain that nothing in the microwave is carrying an electric charge.

To get to the fuse you will have to either remove the microwave casing completely, or remove the facing on your right side. Different machines call for different strategies. Which ever your appliance calls for, you should only have to remove a few screws to get the casing off.

Some manufacturers of microwave ovens are so concerned that you will hurt yourself trying to repair your machine, that they use special screws around the casings which can not be removed with a common screwdriver.

Philosophically, I agree with them. But where there is a will there is a way. You can probably find a screwdriver that fits at your local hardware store.

The oven light bulb is usually located on the same side. If that is true on your microwave, do yourself a favor and replace the bulb at the same time you are working on the fuse.

Removing the fuse should be done without touching any other component in the appliance.

WARNING: Unless you have a great deal of confidence in your technician, go to a hardware store to get the fuse tested to see if it is still good.

Rogue service people will often use two common ploys to take advantage of unsuspecting customers:

1. The service man may tell you that the good fuse is bad, and sell you a new one. You buy it, bring it home. Install it. The microwave doesn't work and you have to bring the micro-wave in for service. When you bring it in, he may fix the problem and put your old fuse back in.

2. The service man may tell you the bad fuse is good. Since that is not the problem, you should bring the microwave oven in for service. He has just proven how "honest" he is, you bring the appliance in, he charges you for a major repair and just replaces the fuse.

In my work with consumers groups I have seen thousands of cases where these techniques have cost unwary consumers over a hundred dollars.

Two ways to get around this. #1, take your fuse in to your local hardware store or parts store to have it checked. #2, find a good service technician and stick with him.

If the fuse does not solve the problem, you have something major wrong with your microwave oven. Major problems tend to create a burnt smell inside the appliance.

If the microwave is 3 to 5 years old, shop around. Find out how much it would cost to buy a replacement. Then take your microwave in to a good qualified service technician, ask him or her how much it will cost to repair and make the decision on repair or replacement.

Chapter 10

DISHWASHERS

PART I: SHOPPING?

FIVE QUICK QUESTIONS TO ASK:

1. **Does this unit have a preheat cycle?** You may not need or want this feature. You'll read more about it in the following chapter.

2. **Does this unit have an energy saver feature?** Sometime you may not need or want the heat on during the drying cycle.

3. **Does it have a plastic or a porcelain tub?** Porcelain may last longer.

4. **Are there interchangeable colored front panels?** Nice feature when redecorating.

5. **What is the water consumption?** The more water it uses, the more it costs to run.

FIVE QUALITY FEATURES TO LOOK FOR:

1. **Porcelain tub.**

2. **Replaceable front panels.**

3. **Ease of operation.**

4. **Ease of D-I-Y repair.**

5. **Low cost of replacement parts.**

   You would not believe how important dishwashers are to the American family. I see the proof every working day. A housewife may be very understanding when a part to the washing machine has to be ordered. She may even be compassionate when the oven is out of action for a week. But let a part be back ordered on a dishwasher and she will call me daily.

   And not just the lady of the house. Husbands hound me, and even singles show a single minded devotion to dishwasher repair when that appliance breaks down.

Dishwashers are also one of the big topics of conversation at my seminars and on my radio shows. I believe that there are three reasons for this:

1. Once an automatic dishwasher enters our lives it saves us so much time and drudgery that it becomes absolutely essential.

2. We use it every day so we see the results of the dishwashers use every day.

3. To be polite, 95% of all users, use it wrong so most of us always think there is something wrong.

If all you were to get out of this book would be to learn how to use a dishwasher properly, it would be a bargain. To see how much of an impact dishwashers have on your life, get yourself a nice cool glass of water, then sit down, relax, read and learn.

Before you fill your glass, hold it up to a light bulb and look at all the scratches. Those scratches are called etching. They are caused by improper dishwasher use.

Getting the proper dishwasher, and making certain that it is installed properly, are also very important factors in your overall happiness with the product.

Unfortunately, given their importance, if there is any product in the major home appliance industry that exemplifies a junk product, it is the American dishwasher. We in the service industry have looked on as manufacturers have put their name on appliances which should never have been allowed into the country.

The problem is plain old fashioned greed. Dishwashers are very big business and some manufacturers will stoop to almost anything to gain the competitive price edge, even at the cost of cheapening their products.

This is not a blanket statement. All teenagers are not beer swilling, pot smoking what-evers. All American dishwashers are not junk. There are some fine old American names out there that make dishwashers that are among the best in the world. Dishwashers that should run for twenty years and never give a problem.

Once again, it is a case of you get what you pay for. If the deal looks too good to be true, it probably is.

When dishwasher shopping, it is extremely important for the consumer to do his or her homework. Read the literature. Study *Consumer Reports*. Which brands are given high ratings on a consistent basis? If you are over eighteen years old, you probably know the names already.

The final step in the successful shopping process is for the consumer to shop like an adult, not a rather greedy child. Wishing doesn't make it so. Quality manufacturers, like quality anything, charge more for their products. They have to. Quality costs, but in the long run, it saves.

THINGS TO THINK ABOUT

As I've already indicated, when you go shopping for an automatic dishwasher, you have to really be on the lookout for quality. In addition, I suggest you also look for simplicity.

The simpler the mechanism, the longer it will last, the easier and less expensive it is to buy and repair. A dishwasher should be able to provide a rinse and hold cycle, a regular wash cycle and a soak and wash cycle, and a "heat off" switch. Anything more is gilding the lily.

Here are a few drawbacks to some of the most popular features:

- I don't like touch pad controls anywhere because they are very expensive to replace and impossible to repair. This is especially true on a dishwasher. It provides a very damp environment that is sure to shorten the life of touch pad controls. You will be much better off if the controls are dial or mechanical push button.

- Automatic features that will start your machine at a preset time (middle of the night, while you're away at work, etc.) may sound like a good idea, but they aren't. Many start off with enough cold water to ruin the dish washing job. I'll explain that more later in the chapter. For now, know that you should not use these features if you want clean dishes. Why pay extra for features you will not use?

- Carefully consider whether you need a preheat cycle on your dishwasher. The preheat cycle heats the water in the bottom of the dishwasher to the temperature of 140° F or hotter. The water must be this temperature if you are going to wash, rinse and sanitize your dishes properly. You don't need this heat cycle if you keep your water tank at 140° F.

There are two opinions on this. On the one side, the National Institute for Burn Medicine, conservation groups and child safety groups say that the water in your water tank should not be heated over 120° F for safety reasons. On the other hand, water has to be heated to 140° F for maximum effectiveness in **either your dishwasher or your washing machine.** The only way you can get 140° F in your washing machine is to have your water tank set at least 140° F.

You can have the best of both worlds. I could never live with myself if one of my children or grand children were seriously injured because of my negligence. I'm sure you are the same. This is why I am making such an issue about water temperature.

They tell me that a small child can have a life threatening scald burn in three seconds or less. The elderly may take longer, but are just as prone to scalding from water that is heated to 140° F.

ScaldSafe™, a breakthrough, space age product, manufactured by Resources Conservation, Inc., can make your home safe from scalding. Resource Conservation, Inc. makes special units that screw into faucets, tubs and showers. They shut off water flow automatically within 300 milliseconds of the time water reaches 114° F. For less than $100.00 you can scald proof every faucet in the house.

These products make it possible to have the hot water you need for cleaning and still keep your family safe. For more information, call Resources Conservation, Inc., 1-800-243-2862. Tell 'em that the Appliance Doctor sent you.

The only other objection there can be to 140° F water is wasting energy in the water tank. I like my water hot. I buy a very good hot water tank, wrap it in an extra thick insulation blanket and forget about it.

You have to decide.

1992 DISHWASHER SALES	
Category	Unit Sales
Built-in	3,618,100
Portable	200,000
Total:	3,819,800

These figures are just to give you a "feel" for the industry. They are not a way of saying "Good," "Better," "Best." They do, however, let you see the relative size of the different players.

WHICH MAKES ARE MOST POPULAR?

1992 Dishwasher Market Share[1]		
Make	Ownership	Market Share
General Electric	General Electric	40%
Whirlpool	Whirlpool	31%
Frigidaire	Electrolux	20%
Maytag	Maytag	8%
Thermadore	Thermadore	1%

---

[1]*Appliance Manufacturer*, February 1993, 18.

COMPARE REPLACEMENT COSTS

BEFORE YOU BUY.

As with every appliance, there is a large variety in the replacement costs of what are essentially the same parts among the different manufacturers. Compare repair and replacement costs of items you will probably have to replace during the service life of your appliance. The three parts that have to be replaced most often on a dishwasher are:

1. The Water Valve

2. The Door Switch

3. The Timer

Part #1: The Water Valve

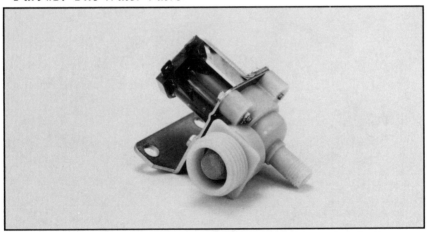

The water valve regulates the flow of water into your dishwasher. Replacement costs run between $20.00 and $50.00. Service calls and labor run between $60.00 and $100.00.

Part #2: The Door Switch

Door switches act like traffic lights. They give the go ahead that the door is sealed, and stop power if the door is opened. This parts cost between $5.00 and $15.00. Labor and a service call brings the cost to between $55.00 and $75.00.

Part #3 The Timer

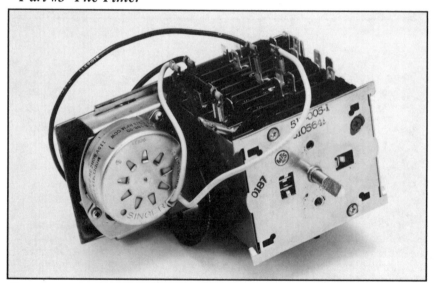

Timers regulate the washing process. Equipment costs vary between $55.00 and $185.00. Labor and a service call should cost between $60.00 and $100.00.

Don't take my word for it. Check out the replacement and service prices on the top two or three contenders on your list at the appliance store. If the retailer does not have a parts & service department, check out the costs at one or two local independent service contractors. Be sure to add an extra hour for diagnostic to the proposed charges. Also inquire as to whether there is an additional service call charge.

Energy Efficiency.

Make sure that your unit has an energy saving feature so you can cut off the heat cycle when you are just rinsing dishes. That way you can just have the blower motor working without the heat.

PART II: SETUP:

A dishwasher can create logistical problems in your kitchen. Many dishwashers are built in. While the design of your kitchen may be perfect while the dishwasher is closed, it may become a perfect nightmare when the dishwasher door is open and you are loading, or unloading the appliance. Kitchen design and dishwasher placement should be laid out with the door open, not closed.

Do's:

Do make sure you read the installation instructions completely before you decide to do it yourself. Dishwasher installation is an art. The dishwasher has to be perfectly level. If it is not you can flood the kitchen. Installation can be done by the homeowner, but do not tackle the project unless you would feel confident doing finished cabinetry in your kitchen.

Do make certain that when the dishwasher has its door open you can still reach and use the drawers and cupboards on either side.

Do make certain that your built-in dishwasher is perfectly level so that the water in the bottom of the dishwasher is level. This is very important if the machine is to give you the best washing action from the bottom spray arm.

The water level in the bottom of the unit is critical to a proper cleaning. This water is used to clean your dishes. The water is channeled by an impeller on top of the motor and forced into the spray arms. In use, the water level should be slightly below the spray arm. If the water is not level and impedes the spray arm, the dishes won't get washed.

When replacing a preexisting dishwasher, do make certain that all the tubing used to drain water is replaced, and that the pipe which supplies the water is copper. Old, worn out tubing and inferior piping will eventually fail and cause water damage. Tearing a new unit out to replace tubes and pipes is very expensive and will tear up your kitchen.

Do consider the condition of your floor before installation. If you add a new sub floor after the new machine is installed you may find that the counter top won't lift and you can't get the leveling legs on the dishwasher up high enough to pull the dishwasher out for repair or replacement.

Do make sure that the dishwasher legs are solidly down on the floor even after you have used screws to anchor the unit to the counter top. If the legs are not firmly on the floor, the weight will actually be born by the small anchoring screws. They will pull out and the weight may shift suddenly, tipping the unit forward. This can be a real mess and has happened to thousands of consumers.

Do take special care when hooking up your new dishwasher to the garbage disposer. Dishwasher drains are usually hooked up to the garbage disposer. Do-It-Yourselfers often install their garbage disposer without removing the drain plug. When the drain hose from the dishwasher is connected to a plugged disposer connector, the dishwasher has no place to drain at the end of the wash cycle and the water goes nowhere.

Unethical service companies will sometimes come out on this type of an emergency call and replace the entire garbage disposer when all that was needed was to take out the plug.

Do install an air gap between the garbage disposer and the dishwasher. This device is designed to prevent raw garbage from feeding back into your dishwasher from the sink area. It sits on the counter and most sinks have a knock out cap where it should be positioned. The proper technique is to run the dishwasher drain hose to the air gap, then run another hose from the air gap to the disposer.

Do add extra insulation around a built-in dishwasher. You will notice the manufacturer has already installed some insulation to deaden the sound of the washing operation. If your kitchen has a lot of wood and Formica or other hard reflective surfaces, extra insulation will pay big dividends in sound control. Before you install the dishwasher, take a trip to your local lumber yard or hardware store and pick up a strip of the blanket type of insulation. It will make your kitchen a much quieter place.

Do make sure your dishwasher has a separate electric circuit. It should not share power with anything. Also, remember the dishwasher is a very damp environment. That means all electrical work should be done in the safest, most water proof manner possible.

PART III: USE:

Remember at the beginning of the chapter when I said that 95% of the people didn't use their dish washers properly. Here are the secret ingredients.

- **Always run the hot water in the sink for three or four minutes before turning on the dishwasher.** If you do not do this the first water into your dishwasher will be cold water that has been sitting in the pipes. This water is critical to the cleaning process. It is necessary for the water temperature to be 140° F for the detergent to dissolve properly and clean and sanitize effectively.

Extremely hot water also leaves less spotting on glassware. Because the hot water dissolves the detergent completely, it does not etch your glassware.

- **Use the minimum amount of soap to do a proper job.** Using too much soap can also cause etching of glassware. The formula for proper soap usage is one teaspoon of powdered soap (I prefer powder) for each grain of hardness in the water.

If your water has 10 grains of hardness, use 10 teaspoons of dishwasher detergent. If you don't know how hard your water is, call your local water company and ask. Most cities with treated water have about 10 grains of hardness. If you have a well, or can't get the information, you can probably get a testing kit from your local hardware store.

Once you know the formula, mark a measuring cup, or better still, find one that holds the exact amount and use it for your dishwasher detergent exclusively.

- **Never store your powdered dish washing detergent under the sink.** Under the sink is the most humid spot in your house. The dry detergent absorbs water like a sponge. The humid conditions make the detergent solidify into rock hard chunks which never dissolve properly and create havoc on your fine china and glassware.

The proper way to store dish washing detergent is in a plastic container with an air tight lid on a shelf far from the sink.

- **Always rinse the dishes before you put them in the dishwasher.** Some of the dishwasher manufacturers advertise that their super dooper machines rinse the dishes for you. They will. The only problem is that some of this waste can plug up the filters or impede water flow through the spray ports.

A dishwasher is not a garbage disposer. It has not been designed to act like a garbage disposer. You should not expect it to act like one. If you listen to the advertising claims instead of me, that's OK. But remember, you, not me or the manufacturer, will be stuck with the service call.

- **Load the dishwasher properly.** Proper loading is very important to the dishwasher's ability to clean. If you place upside down bowls in the bottom rack, the water spraying from the bottom arm can deflect into the water reservoir at the bottom of the dishwasher and cause a wave. This can create a door leak as well as ineffective cleaning action.

PART IV: MAINTENANCE:

Daily:

Inspect the dishwasher after each use. If you see sediment accumulating around filters or at the bottom of the dishwasher, clean thoroughly.

Monthly:

Lift up the bottom spray arm (it may just lift off) and inspect to see that no sediment is plugging up the holes on the spray arm mechanism.

Give your dishwasher a refreshing drink of Tang® every month or two. I, personally, have never even tasted Tang®. Although a number of astronauts swear by the stuff. I do know that it will give your dishwasher a quick energy boost.

Many customers who have come to me complaining about leaky dishwasher doors have solved the problem with Tang. The secret is that Tang in your dishwasher will clear away all the undissolved soap which coats the impellers, seals and surfaces of everything. Once the seals get coated, they start to harden. As soon as they harden they become unable to seal the water in.

The technique is to dump an entire one pint jar of Tang into the bottom of an empty dishwasher. Preheat the water as if it were a regular wash. Then, run the dishwasher through its regular cycle.

One warning: If you have leaky door seals, check to see if the Tang discolors your flooring before trying this. If you have kitchen carpeting the Tang may leave a very hard to remove stain.

ATTENTION ALL COTTAGERS AND RETIREES:

When you leave on a trip:

The motor seal on your dishwasher should be kept moist at all times. If the seals dry up on the motor shaft, water can leak down the shaft and ruin the motor, causing a very expensive repair.

If you are going to be gone for more than one month, have someone you trust go to your house and pour two quarts of water into your dishwasher every thirty days.

PART V: TROUBLE SHOOTING

PROBLEM: The racks in my dishwasher have begun to rust and are starting to stain my china.

Dishwasher racks are coated with a rubber like coating to protect your dishes. Up until very recently, when the rubber wore off the racks and the metal began to rust, there was no solution other than to replace the rack no matter how structurally sound it was.

Over the years, dishwasher racks have become very expensive to replace. Prices of $80.00 per rack are not uncommon.

Thanks to Maytag and the Whirlpool Co. there is now a cost efficient solution. Both companies have come out with a rack repair kit. The little bottle of coating comes with a self applicator.

Now, all you have to do to solve the problem is to clean off all the rust with an emery board, wipe away all dust particles, and apply a new coating from the self applicating bottle. The final result is just like the original.

PROBLEM: My dishes aren't getting clean.

Dirty dishes can be caused by the spray arms not turning. The first thing to do is check to see that the spray arms are working and that the water level is correct at the bottom of you dishwasher.

Make sure the dishwasher is empty. Look down and check the exact location of the bottom spray arm. Close the door and run the wash cycle for three or four minutes.

Shut off the machine and open the door. Check the location of the spray arm. It should show signs of having moved. If it hasn't check the base of the dishwasher. The water should be perfectly level and about 1/2" below the bottom spray arm. Twirl the spray arm with your hand gently. Check to see that it is not hitting the water.

If it is running freely, heave a sigh of relief, then lift up the spray arm (technically it's called an impeller arm) and inspect the center bearing or nut. If it shows signs of wear replace it.

OK JOE, Every thing here is fine. Now what do I do? The Dishes still are not clean.

Make sure that all the water is draining out after the wash cycle. See the answer to the problem "The Dishwasher will not drain" on the next page. If you are washing dishes with dirty water because of a drain problem, you'll never get the dishes clean.

If all this doesn't help, it's time to call your friendly service technician.

PROBLEM: The dishwasher is dead. It just doesn't run.

After you have made sure that the circuit breaker has not blown and that you have power to the unit check the door switch. The dishwasher door switch is activated by locking the door. It is usually accessible by removing a few screws.

If that is OK, grab the flashlight and check the wiring thoroughly. The dishwasher is a very humid environment. It is common for a wire to break. If you find a broken, or loose wire, turn off the power and replace the wire, or call an electrician.

PROBLEM: The water does not come into the dishwasher.

The most common reason for this is that there is a problem with the fill valve under the unit. To check this out, remove the bottom kick panel. The fill line will lead directly to the fill valve. Shut off the water supply, disconnect the fill valve and have it checked out at your local parts store.

If the fill valve is good, check the float switch.

Fill valve.

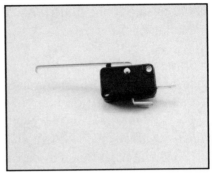

Float switch.

The float switch may be defective and need to be replaced, or the float inside the dishwasher may be stuck in the up position.

PROBLEM: The dishwasher will not drain.

Remember when I told you to rinse the dishes before putting them in the dishwasher? This problem is usually caused by sloppy pre-rinse. OK, OK, I'll stop complaining. I just had to get it off my chest.

If your dishwasher has an air gap and hooks up to the garbage disposer, there are two areas to check. The first place to look is the air gap. It should be disassembled and cleaned. Remove the cap on the sink and run a small baby bottle brush up and down inside the stem to clean it.

The other place to check is the spout on the garbage disposer that hooks up to the drain hose. Take off the drain hose and clean the inside of the spout.

Some makes of dishwashers have a solenoid valve located underneath the dishwasher that connects to the drain line.

The solenoid may have a food particle preventing it from opening. Take off the solenoid valve. Take it apart to clean it, or take it to your local parts outlet to check if the solenoid is working properly.

PROBLEM: The dishwasher drains while washing.

This is usually caused by a food particle jamming the drain solenoid flapper in the open position. Take it apart and clean it thoroughly. Replace the solenoid. The dishwasher should work fine now.

PROBLEM: Small pieces of broken glass have chewed up the motor impellers on my dishwasher.

Bad news. Damaged motor impellers can only be replaced on a few makes. If you can take the impeller off easily, take it into the parts outlet. Other models will have to have the entire pump and motor replaced. Call a trustworthy service contractor for advice.

PROBLEM: The door springs on my dishwasher have broken.

Don't use them for a shelf next time. OK?

Broken door springs will cause the door to come down hard and can do serious injury to the machine or even tip it over. The Do-It-Yourselfer can replace the door springs by removing the lower panel for easy access.

PROBLEM: The timer went out.

The timer should be treated with gentle care when setting it and **should never be turned while the dishwasher is in operation.**

This is a very expensive part. Before replacing it, remove the panel on which it is located and try spraying the inner contacts with electronic cleaner. If that doesn't work, I'm sorry but you just bought yourself a new timer.

PROBLEM: The door gaskets are torn and leaking.

If the door gaskets are torn, they have to be replaced. If they are just hardened, but not actually leaking, try giving them a drink of Tang (see earlier tip). Clean them thoroughly. Try spraying on a light coat of silicone, to make them flexible. Then go through the wash cycle and see if the problem is solved. If it is, you saved yourself some money.

If not, or if inspection shows that the door gaskets are torn in any location, they have to be replaced. This is a relatively easy thing to do if you take a careful look at the dishwasher door.

Go down to your local parts supplier and pick up door gaskets for the exact model dishwasher. When you do the actual installation, spray a little lubricant onto the area to which you are going to fit the gasket. It will make the job a lot easier.

Chapter 11

GARBAGE DISPOSERS

PART I: SHOPPING?

FIVE QUICK QUESTIONS TO ASK:

1. **Will it fit?** Not all garbage disposers are the same size. Make sure the one you choose will fit under your sink.

2. **Can I install it myself?** Is the disposer set up for easy installation and are there good, clear directions.

3. **What can't I put into this unit?** A grape seed will give some garbage disposers problems. Others can grind up bolts.

4. **What is the horsepower?** Don't confuse motor power with quality. The quality depends upon the cutter blades, not the power of the unit.

5. **How do I activate it?**

QUALITY FEATURES TO LOOK FOR:

1. Good Warranty.

2. Easy clearing.

3. Easy to follow installation instructions.

4. "Heavy duty" or "Comercial grade" classification.

A War story and a recommendation.

Almost.

I was planning to do something in this chapter that I have not done in any other portion of the book. I was going to recommend a particular product. This is the type of advice that I would give you if we were having a quiet talk over a cup of coffee before you went appliance shopping.

For years I had a live display of a Maytag disposer in my store. I had a coffee can filled with one inch nails sitting beside the disposer. As part of the demonstration, I would turn on the disposer and thrown in hands full of nails.

Hooked up to the disposer was a plastic container which would catch the nail shavings after I had run them through the disposer.

After using this garbage disposer as a demonstrator in my store for over a year, I was visited by a Maytag Vice President. I explained to him that I did not see how it was possible for the disposer to be used in these demonstrations without doing tremendous damage to the unit.

The vice president told me that he thought this was probably the highest quality product the company made. If you know Maytag's reputation for quality that is saying a lot. Because of my concern, he said he would take the product apart, and if the cutters had any nicks or signs of undo wear and tear, the factory would give me a brand new disposer.

He took the machine apart in front of me. The cutters had no wear. The inner parts looked almost new. The quality of construction was the best that I had ever seen and made a true believer out of me.

I have had several different name brand disposers in my lifetime. No other residential disposer I know could do that job.

Unfortunately, one day before this book was scheduled to go to press, I learned that Maytag had shut down their garbage disposer line and stopped making their superior product.

Although they made the best garbage disposer, it was also, very naturally, the most expensive. Sales had dropped to only 2% of the market and they could not afford to keep the line going. I am sorry to say this, but this is another case in which the overprice conscious American consumer is going to get exactly what he/she is willing to pay for.

You can get a disposer today for anywhere from $39.00 to $250.00. You get what you pay for. The cheaper the disposer, the more careful you have to be about what you put into it. With a cheap unit, corn husks, potato peelings and fibrous materials will cause serious problems.

WHICH MAKES ARE MOST POPULAR?

1992 Garbage Disposer Sales[1]	
Approximately 4,064,000 Total Units Sold	
Make	**Market Share**
In-Sink-Erator	65%
Electrolux (Anaheim)	17%
Waste King	10%
Kitchen Aid	2%
Matag	2%
Watertown Metal Prods.	2%

My suggestion is to buy the most heavy duty product you can find. Look for terms like "heavy duty" and "commercial grade."

---

[1]*Appliance Manufacturer*, February 1993, 18.

If you have a top quality disposer in your kitchen, you will never have to put waste food in a trash container to create odors and draw rats. To me, getting the very best garbage disposer money can buy is a very worthwhile investment. I am sorry that you will no longer be able to get the best. What you buy is up to you.

PART II: SETUP:

A garbage disposer is relatively easy for the Do-It-Yourselfer to install himself or herself. Just follow the directions that come with the garbage disposer. **Make sure you have taken out the drain plug if a dishwasher is being hooked up to the disposer.** If a dishwasher is not being hooked up to the unit, leave the drain blocked.

PART III: USE:

Always run cold water for one or two minutes after you have shut off the disposer. This is very important to keeping the drain clear.

Something as small as a small metallic tie down, like those you get on a loaf of bread, is enough to jam a disposer, especially one of the cheaper models.

PART IV: MAINTENANCE:

Daily:

Remember to keep the cold water running for at least one minute after you have turned off the garbage disposer **every time.**

Be very careful to only use non-caustic drain cleaners when you clear the drain. Lye based drain cleaners can ruin the disposers motor seals and rubber parts.

I've told my radio listeners my own secret method of cleaning plugged drains and it has been getting rave reviews for years. It is not sophisticated, but it's easy on the disposer and pipes and might work for you, too.

Pour a cup full of baking soda into the drain. Then slowly pour in a quart of white vinegar. Put the stopper in the drain hole and fill the sink with water.

Let stand for one hour. Pull the stopper from the drain. The water usually flows boom, boom, bam, right down the drain.

Monthly:

A plumber friend of mine, Art Cameron, always told me that most plugged drains could be eliminated by running hot water through the drain for ten minutes once a month.

I recommend filling the entire disposer with ice cubes and leaving them sit for half an hour. The cold cubes solidify the grease deposits plugging the inner drain holes. These solid glob-ules of grease are then washed away when you turn on the water and disposer.

PART V: TROUBLE SHOOTING

PROBLEM: The garbage disposer started running then jammed.

Follow the technique printed in your disposer operating instructions. There is a big nut under most disposers that can be used to turn the rotor blades. Turn off the unit and use the wrench that came with your garbage disposer to turn the rotor counter clockwise. If that doesn't work, try to turn the rotor from the top with a long handled screwdriver or a tire iron.

Once you have rotated the works, push the reset button on the bottom of the disposer under the sink.

If it still doesn't work after you have turned the power back on, check to see if your have burned out a fuse or tripped the circuit breaker.

If the disposer is still stuck, turn off the electricity again and shine a flash light into the disposer cavity. Locate what is stuck and try to pull it out with a pair of needle nosed pliers. Never use your bare hand.

Chapter 12

WASHING MACHINES

PART I: SHOPPING?

FIVE QUICK QUESTIONS TO ASK:

1. **What is the life expectancy of this machine?** Anything less than fourteen years is unacceptable. Ask to see the life expectancy claim in print.

2. **What is the model year of this machine?** Many high volume stores are able to sell at low prices because they are selling outdated equipment. There is nothing wrong with buying last year's equipment (it may even be a better machine), but you should know what you are getting.

3. **What is the load size?** Is it the proper size for your family's needs.

4. **What is the rinsing capability?** How thorough a job does it do getting the soap out of the clothing?

5. **What is the water usage?** Water costs. The more used, the more expensive.

FIVE QUALITY FEATURES TO LOOK FOR:

1. **Simple manual not touch pad controls.**

2. **Out of balance switch.**

3. **Manual clean filters.**

4. **Highly effective rinse cycle.** Many people become allergic to the chemicals in soap that has not been rinsed from the clothing. I prefer a spray type rinse during the spin cycle.

5. **How easy is the machine to repair?** Is it easy to get into? Does a really good repair manual come with the machine, or is there one available for just a little money?

THINGS TO THINK ABOUT

I have met thousands of consumers throughout my career. Many have talked to me about their washing machines. Many were complaining. Dishwashers aside, I don't think there is another product which causes so many consumer complaints.

This is because the washing machine is so important to us. When it stops working it makes a big impact on our lives. If we feel that we have been badly treated, or that the machine did not live up to its cost and promise, you can rest assured that we'll have bad feelings toward the manufacturer and tell people about it for a long time.

All Americans want the newest and best. But the newest and best technology always costs more and sometimes is not even needed.

For instance, ninety-five percent of the time most families wash full loads of clothes. Why do you need four or five different wash sizes?

WHICH MAKES ARE MOST POPULAR?

1992 Washing Machine Market Share[1]		
Total Sales: 6,322,000		
Make	**Ownership**	**Market Share**
Whirlpool	same	52%
Maytag	same	17%
General Electric	same	16%
Amana, Speed Queen	Raytheon	4%

SHOPPING TIPS

Based on my many years of experience in the service business, I believe that the best four manufacturers of washing machines today, in alphabetical order, are Amana, General Electric, Maytag and Speed Queen.

---

[1]*Appliance Manufacturer*, February 1993, 18.

This does not mean that they never make mistakes or never sell equipment that is not state of the art. It means that year in, year out, they have made a reliable product. It also does not mean that no other manufacturer makes a quality product.

No matter what the brand name, be very careful about selecting the floor special. I believe that many base models are basically "bait 'n switch" products, very cheaply made, designed to provide price but not performance. Even some of the best manufacturers will stoop to this practice from time to time so that they can give their retailers a super competitive advertising item.

Try to determine the average estimated service life of the product. The typical washing machine should last fourteen years. If you only get seven or eight years, you would be better off paying a hundred dollars more and getting a fourteen year service life.

If you are really interested, ask the salesman to take off the front of the lower priced washing machine, and the front of a mid or high priced machine by the same manufacturer. Are the machines noticeably different inside? Is the low priced machine of demonstrably cheaper construction (it shouldn't be)?

If the salesman will not, or can not, take off the front side of the machine, to allow you to look at the inner construction, ask yourself if you would buy a car from an automobile dealership where they wouldn't lift the hood and let you look at the engine, or from a salesman who couldn't find the oil dip stick?

When you go shopping, ask yourself if color is really important. If it is not of life and death concern, buy white. If you feel color is an important consideration, ask the millions of consumer who, at one time or another, bought brown, green, pink, or any one of many different colors the industry has had over the years.

If you buy a washer and dryer at the same time, the probability is that you will have to replace the washer before the dryer. When the time comes to replace the washer, you will most probably not be able to match the dryer color. You will eventually be stuck with either a discordant color scheme, or having to throw out a perfectly good dryer, so that washer and dryer match.

Manufacturers change colors every few years. Many people believe that this is just so that consumers can't find a replacement and have to buy two new appliances, instead of one. This probably isn't chicanery on the part of the companies.

Since washing machines stay pretty much the same (we haven't had a major new advancement in twenty years), color is used as a major element to create excitement in new model. Design teams keep changing the least popular colors hoping for one that will make a major sales impact. Naturally, if fate has its way, the color you need will be the one they canceled.

Bear in mind that the fancier the machine is, the more it will cost. Simplicity is a virtue. If you have an average size family, you probably need the following features:

Three temperature settings: hot, medium and cold. Cold water is good for rinsing. Hot is best for washing. Medium may be needed for delicate fabrics. Never wash with cold water. If the fabric is that delicate, use a product like Woolite® and hand wash.

Two speed settings: Regular and delicate.

One or two wash size settings: Most families would be better off if you just used the large load setting, but if you only have a couple of pieces a small or medium load setting is nice. If there are only one or two of you in the family, why do you need more than a regular size (cheaper) tub?

Any other settings are of little practical value.

Manual buttons and dials. Electronic touch pad controls look nice and make you feel like you're in the 21st Century. They are very expensive to replace and do not have a track record for long lasting reliability. I have had a lot of customers who, once they found out how expensive the replacement electronic controls were, preferred to buy a brand new washing machine with traditional controls.

Don't buy a larger tub than necessary. There are only two different tub sizes, regular and extra large. The extra large tub only cleans two pounds more clothing and can cost you a lot more money. When you buy a washer with a large tub you usually get stuck with a lot of added features.

Energy Efficiency. With a washing machine, you are the prime factor in determining the energy efficiency. That's because the efficiency stems from the temperature and the amount of water you use.

The hot water tank is the prime user of energy. Use a lot of hot water when you wash the clothes and the bill goes up, the energy efficiency goes down. Use small amounts of cold water and energy efficiency sky rockets. The only problem with this is that generally speaking, the hotter the water, the better the cleaning action. As a general rule, the more water you use, the better the rinse. Only you can decide whether energy efficiency or cleaning power is more important.

As I have recommended throughout this book your shopping is not done when you have gotten what appears to be a good deal on a washer. You have to compare repair and replacement costs. The parts that have to be replaced most often on a washer are:

1. The water level pressure switch

2. The water valve

3. The water pump

If the appliance retailer at which you are shopping has a parts department, check out the retail costs of these parts at your retailer. If the retailer does not have a parts & service department, check at a parts store.

Part #1: The Water Level Pressure Switch

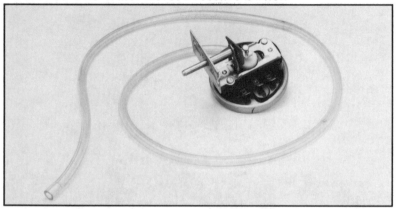

The water level pressure switch is what translates your control panel command into reality as you change the setting from small to large or medium load . The pressure switch costs between $18.00 and $50.00. Add an extra $60.00 to $100.00 for the service call and installation.

Part #2: The Water Valve

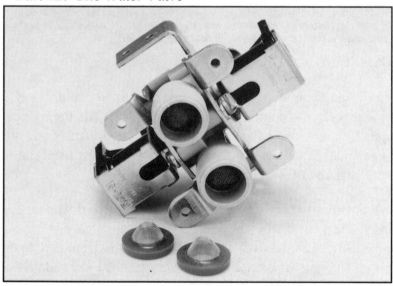

The water valve connects and regulates the hot and cold water hoses. It regulates the water temperature. A generic water valve costs around $20.00. Branded valves are usually much higher. The service call and installation will add about $60.00 to $150.00.

Part #3 The Water Pump

The water pump is either belt driven or direct drive and pumps the water out of the washing machine. Pump prices range from $20.00 to $50.00. A service call and installation can add between $60 and $150.00.

Service Costs

For those of you who do not have the time to do the job itself, it is very important to compare both the actual parts and the service charges for these items. Do not rely on my figures. They come from personal experience and may not apply to your part of the country or brand of washer.

Ask the time and labor costs for these items at your Appliance Retailer. Then check out the same costs at local independent service contractors. Always add an extra hour for diagnostic to the proposed charges. Also inquire as to whether there is an additional service call charge.

PART II: SETUP:

Do's: (These tips may make me sound like a little old lady. Please believe me, I have witnessed a thousand horror stories associated with people not following these basic instructions.)

Do make certain that the washing machine is absolutely level. That does not mean that it looks level, that means that you've taken out a level and assured yourself that the floor is perfect. If uneven, or slanted, rebuild the base to provide a firm, level foundation. Use the adjustment screws at the base of the machine only for minor corrections. They should really be screwed in all the way to provide a firm foundation.

Do install the washing machine on cement, or on a base that is as solid as cement. I know that many people want the washer on the first or second floor. That makes good sense from the usage point of view. However, if you do this, realize that the floor should be especially reinforced under the washer and dryer. Most houses today are not built solidly enough to provide a movement free base for the equipment. If the floor starts "bouncing" in time with the washer rotation, major injury to the washer may result.

Do hope that your guardian angel is looking after you if you install the washing machine on an above ground floor. When something goes wrong, washing machines sometimes cause flooding conditions. This is a big inconvenience in the basement. It can be a major tragedy on the first or second floor.

If your washing machine is on the second floor, take a look at what is under it on the first floor. Let me be the first to tell you, that spot is not the ideal location for priceless antiques, a grand piano, or a $3000.00 sofa. Make sure your homeowner's insurance policy covers your rugs and furniture for water damage.

Michael Hyman, one of Detroit's quality builders and General Manager of the Fairway Construction Company, is so concerned about this water overflow problem that when his company does a remodeling job that includes a second floor laundry room, they install a basin under the washer. The basin is built into the floor and has a drain leading to one of the drain pipes on the lower level.

His idea makes a lot of sense and I recommend it to you.

When replacing a prior washer, do make sure you use the new hose connectors which come with the machine. Do not reuse the old hoses from your old machine. The hose connectors are your machines lifeline to the hot and cold water you need to clean clothes. The water taps at the other end of those hoses are turned on high. If a hose bursts, your house will be flooded.

Some retailers remove the hose connectors from the washing machine box and sell them as parts. You bought new hose connectors as part of the washing machine. The manufacturer shipped new hose connectors as part of the machine. Demand that the retailer give you new hose connectors. You paid for them.

Do make sure the water faucets to which the washing machine is connected are in perfect condition. A faucet leak could cause a flood. The faucets are there for a reason. Very few people do it, but the faucets should be turned on before doing the wash, and off after you have finished doing washing for the day. Not doing this keeps continuous water pressure on the hose connectors, a good way to induce eventual hose failure.

Do make certain that the drain hose releases at a higher elevation than the top of the water in the washing machine. If the release is not higher, gravity drainage will set in and your machine will be constantly filling. Connect the drain hose to a stand pipe if necessary. But do this cautiously. If the hose fits into the opening too tightly, you can create a vacuum effect that will cause service problems.

If you install the washing machine yourself, do read the installation instructions and the service manual carefully.

If you have the washing machine installed by a plumber, do watch him or her like a hawk. He can teach you a hundred things while he is installing the machine. You want to take special care to learn how to open up and do minor service on the equipment.

Don'ts:

Do not use old connector hoses.

Do not install the washer out of level.

Do not over extend base screws.

Do not use abrasive cleaners on the consoles.

Do not be rough on the timer control.

Do not turn timer control backwards.

PART III: USE:

Never overload the washing machine! Ask any service professional, this is the prime cause for washing machine failure. You may think you are saving a little time, or a little soap.

Here is what you are really doing:

- You are causing undo strain on all the mechanical parts.

- You are not permitting enough water to wash through the clothing. While cleaning, this means that enough detergent is not getting to the clothing to do a good job. While rinsing, it means that enough clear water is not getting to the clothing to rise away the detergent.

- You are causing a tremendous amount of extra wear and tear on your clothing. The cloth should be rubbing against water, not other clothing.

- You are reducing the service life of your washer by three or four years.

Instead of overloading the washing machine, make a practice of under loading the machine. All it is costing you is a little extra water and a little extra time. For the cleanest, brightest clothing, a good rule of thumb is: two loads are better than one.

Use the hottest water your fabric will allow. The hotter the water, the more active your detergent will be. The more active the detergent, the less you have to use and the cleaner your clothing will be.

Check the warm water cycle temperature with a cooking thermometer. **Never let the warm water cycle be lower than 100° F.** Any lower and your clothes won't clean. Adjust the hot and cold water valves to provide the proper hot water input. You will have to recheck the temperatures and readjust the water every winter.

Hopefully you have taken my advice and gotten a machine with manual controls, usually dials for the type of wash, etc. No matter what type of controls you have, follow this rule: **Never move the dials while the machine is running.** Switching the machine from one setting to another during the cycle will give the machine a "nervous breakdown."

Even with mechanical dials it is easy to get in trouble. Controls go bad quite often and it is almost always the fault of the consumer. **Never turn the dials fast. Never turn the dials backward or you are sure to break something.**

My advice on moving a washer from one location to another is simple: Don't.

Well, maybe that is a little drastic. What I mean is that if you want to move a washer from here to there, you really should take about 24 hours off to think about it.

Once a washing machine is leveled and set up, moving it to another location can cause big problems after reinstallation. When moving it to your new home, remember, to function properly the washing machine must be very solid and perfectly level. Jarring the machine while moving, could upset the delicate balance of the machine and break some parts.

Above all: Never lay a washing machine on its side. Just one second of that is enough to break stability parts or plastic tub parts that will ruin the washer and cause flooding in the laundry room.

One final note about washing machine operation:

Washing machines are usually located in basements. Basements are the areas in the house most prone to be damp or flooded.

Please:

If there is water on the floor, do not try to use the washing machine. Water and electricity do not mix. It could literally kill you!

PART IV: MAINTENANCE:

Very little maintenance is needed on a washing machine. It's a good idea to wipe your washing machine down thoroughly at least once a week. If you spill detergent, clean it up immediately. Do not let your equipment get gunked up with detergent, etc.

Twice a year clean out your machine with two quarts of white vinegar in a full tub full of hot water. Let the washing machine run through the entire cycle. It will look shiny and new when the cycle is completed.

PART V: TROUBLE SHOOTING

A washing machine is basically just a tub within a tub, within a square metal box. It has a motor attached to the transmission by a belt or direct drive attachment. The transmission will move the agitator back and forth, as well as spin the inner tub. There is also a pump to remove the water when the job is done.

If all the manufacturers put the same parts in the same places, and all the various parts looked like their counterparts on competitive machines, telling you how to fix a washing machine would be a snap. Unfortunately, the parts don't all look the same and they are not situated in the same place. Therefore, please don't try to repair a washing machine without that particular brand's service manual.

Many publishing companies sell big hard covered repair books. They give good general information, but I suggest that you get the exact manual for the exact piece of equipment you own. That way when you are in the middle of a job, you'll usually have a picture of the exact part you are looking for and won't have to play twenty questions with yourself. "Is this the part, or is it the thing-of-a-magig over there?"

Remember "knowledge is power." Buy the manual even if you never expect to do any repair work yourself. If you look up the repair before a repair person does the job, you'll see step by step what he or she should be doing. You'll get a pretty good idea how long the job should take and you can be an aware consumer and speak knowledgeably about the repair.

I am going to give you some very basic instruction and list the jobs I think most people can do themselves, plus give you a few tips I've learned over the years.

PROBLEM: My washing machine has stopped, what do I do first?

First things you want to do is check to see that the washer isn't smarter than you are. Some washers automatically shut off if the load is too heavy.

Next, check that the circuit breaker hasn't popped or that some little gremlin has not pulled the plug out of its socket.

PROBLEM: The timer on my washer has stopped. What do I do?

In your situation I'd pray a lot. Remember how I told you that timers on a washing machine were very delicate **and very expensive**? Now maybe you'll believe old Joe knows what he is talking about.

OK. Enough of the "I told you sos". First thing you do is pull the plug on the machine and open up the console. See if there is anything noticeably wrong, a loose part, etc. If everything is together (it usually is), clean everything thoroughly. Then spray all the moving parts with a good lubricant. Close the console back up, plug the machine back in, and pray. Try the switch and see if it works.

If it does, you're golden. Use more care next time. Remember, slow and gentle wins the race. Never jamb the dials or turn them backwards. Always turn in a gentle clockwise motion.

If the controls still don't work, call your local parts supplier and discuss the problem with him. See how much parts replacement run. Hold on to your wallet, some washer controls can easily cost $150.00.

PROBLEM: The water level setting on my washing machine is out of whack, no matter what the setting, I get a full load of water.

The water level pressure switch has probably gone out. This part is located immediately behind the knob which indicates water level setting on the console. When you open the console you will see that the switch is connected to a small hose that goes down to the bottom of the tub.

As the tub fills, the hose fills as well, increasing the air pressure at the top of the hose. When the tub has been filled to the desired amount, the air pressure in the hose has been built up to a predetermined amount, triggering the switch and turning off the water.

The entire system works great until the hose or the air pressure switch starts letting air escape. When that happens the tub could continue filling until your house floats away. Since this part could fail at any time, it is really a good idea to stay nearby while the washing machine is operating.

PROBLEM: The water in my washing machine is either too hot, or too cold.

Same solution to both problems. Usually the problem is that either the cold or the hot water valve has gone bad. To find out which side of the valve has failed, hold a small metal nail on top of the coil. You will feel a slight magnetic pull on one coil. That coil is good. The coil that demonstrates no magnetic pull is dead and has to be replaced. The coil and water valve assembly, should cost you in the area of $20.00.

If you feel the magnetic pull on both the hot and cold water coils, there is a good chance that the screen inside one valve have become plugged and is either slowing or preventing water from going through the valve. This is especially common with the hot water valve because of sediment from the hot water tank.

The photo in the replacement parts section of this chapter shows the valve with the screens already pulled out. Simply remove the screens with a small pair of needle nose pliers, clean and replace.

PROBLEM: The water is not going out of the washing machine.

That's usually a sign that the water pump has to be replaced. There is also a possibility that something has lodged in the pump and is keeping it from functioning.

The first thing you have to do is remove the water from the washing machine. In many cases simply lowering the drain hose to the floor will permit the water to flow out of the unit. Please check that there is a floor drain nearby before doing this. If that doesn't work you will have to bail out the tub, or use your garage wet/dry vacuum to pull the water out of the tub. Keep in mind that whatever technique you use, some water will remain and will come out when you remove the pump. It is wise to place two or three heavy bath towels under the pump during removal.

Disconnect the water hoses from the pump and look inside the openings with a flashlight. If you see anything lodged in there, pull it out. You have probably just saved yourself the price of a service call and a water pump.

If you can't see any obstruction, no problem. Water pumps are easy to replace. Just disconnect the pump and take it in to your parts supplier. Then connect the new pump and let'er rip.

You saved yourself a $150.00 service call.

PROBLEM: The agitator has stopped working.

Sometimes this means the belt which drives the transmission is broken. Other times it means that the agitator itself is stripped. The splines at the top of the agitator can be inspected by you once you remove it.

Belts are generally replaceable, but some brands can be very time consuming. A Whirlpool washer belt is especially tough to do and comes with instructions which must be followed to the letter.

Some other manufacturers have made their belts quite easy to replace and you definitely should give it a go. Still make sure you get the printed instructions from your parts supplier.

One final note before starting this repair. Make sure your will is up to date. You are going to be a lot older before you get done.

PROBLEM: My basement flooded and the washing machine got wet.

Motors on appliances have to be completely dried out before they can be used. Thousands of electric motors that could have been saved are destroyed every year.

When the basement is thoroughly dry, pull the plugs on your appliances. Open your washer and dryer and let them air dry. A fan can be a lot of help here.

Finish drying with a hair dryer. Make certain the electric motors are dryer than toast, then double it.

If your electric motor and the rest of the appliance is completely dry, you should be able to start using the washer with no ill effects.

Chapter 13

CLOTHES DRYERS

PART 1: SHOPPING?

FIVE QUICK QUESTIONS TO ASK:

1. What is the drum size?

2. Which way does the door open?

3. How hard is the drum belt to replace?

4. Where does the vent line hook up?

5. What exactly does the warranty cover?

FIVE QUALITY FEATURES TO LOOK FOR:

1. **Easy to understand mechanical controls.**

2. **Automatic drying timer.**

3. **Stationary interior rack for sweaters, tennis shoes, etc.**

4. **Drum light.**

5. **Press care feature** (rotates drum periodically at end of permanent press cycle so that wrinkles will not set).

Let's be honest. No matter what I say, you are probably going to buy the same brand dryer as your washing machine. They are a matched set. The only problem is that although you buy then at the same time, they will probably have to be replaced at different times.

Nothing wrong with that. But be careful about color selection when buying the original equipment. If you buy any color other than white, you will have a very hard time matching colors ten or fifteen years from now. As a cost conscious consumer that means that you would be wise to buy white. Your big choice with a dryer is whether to buy gas or electric. If you are already hooked up for gas, gas dryers cost more to purchase but less than electric to operate.

Gas dryers, use gas to supply the drying heat. Electric dryers use electricity. Even gas dryers still use electricity to power the dryer's electric motor and controls.

I call clothes dryers "the metal boxes into which we throw our clothes for the purpose of catching fire, *'almost.'*" Think about it. Isn't that exactly what we are doing?

To let you know just how close to burning those clothes are, let me give you this one piece of vital information: The US Product Safety Commission reports that 15,000 house fires are started by clothes dryers. And that number is just the *reported* number of house fires. My personal belief is that if we added in all the fires that were not reported by the homeowner, we could double that figure.

With all these fires going on, it stands to reason that there has to be a staggering amount of personal misery, burns, scarring and death associated with the fires. I have not got a hard figure on the pain, suffering and death involved.

In addition to all the heartache this has to be costing the insurance companies untold millions of dollars. It makes me wonder why no government agencies, insurance companies, or organizations like Underwriters Laboratories have not gotten more actively involved with this.

Folks, apparently you are on your own on this. Let me tell you in plain English that the biggest enemy you have in a clothes dryer is lint. Lint will plug up the venting, reduce the efficiency of your dryer, increase your energy bill, cause expensive service calls and can catch fire.

Lint is creating millions and millions of dollars of extra business for the service industry. It doesn't have to be that way. Your dryer can be safe. All you have to do is maintain the product properly. Please read the maintenance section of this chapter very carefully and follow my directions to the letter. It could save you hundreds of dollars in service calls, your house and possibly your life and that of your family.

Some dryers will only last three to five years before they develop serious service problems. Before you buy a dryer do your homework. Read *Consumer's Report* and make sure you are buying a good machine.

THINGS TO THINK ABOUT

The clothes dryer is a fairly cut and dried, easy to understand machine. As long as you keep it clean and do not over load it, your dryer should give you years of use.

Fancy electronic controls look good and do actually speed drying time a little. However, they are far more delicate and very expensive to replace. I much prefer the old fashioned standard timers that we could count on not to give us a problem for twenty years or more.

1992 DRYER SALES[1]	
Type	**Number of Units**
Gas	1,153,700
Electric	3,563,000
Total	4,716,700

[1]*Appliance Manufacturer*, February 1993, 16.

WHICH MAKES ARE MOST POPULAR?

1992 Electric Dryer Market Share[2]		
Make	**Ownership**	**Market Share**
Whirlpool	same	52%
General Electric	same	18%
Norge & Maytag	Maytag	15%
Frigidaire	Electrolux	12%
Speed Queen	Raytheon	3%

SHOPPING TIPS

The dryer is usually the "companion" of the washing machine. Therefore, unless you are purchasing a replacement, it is very probable that you are going to buy the same brand of dryer as washer.

The costs I show below are for demonstration purposes only. They have some pretty wide ranges. These costs are very important to the Do-It-Yourselfer and the Buy-It-Yourselfer. Always check both the parts and service costs in your local area before you buy an appliance. They may give you a whole new out look on what is really the best buy.

[2]*Appliance Manufacturer*, February 1993, 18.

The three parts that have to be replaced most often on a Dryer are:

1. Drum Belt

2. Element

3. Thermostat

Part #1: The Drum Belt

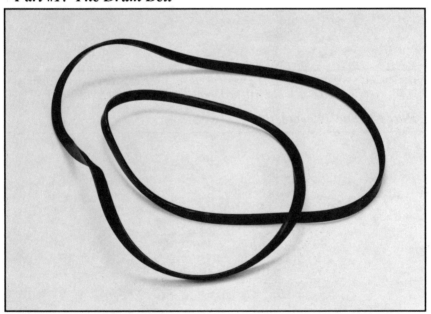

The drum belt goes around the dryer drum and attaches to the motor. When the motor runs, the drum turns. Improper venting of the dryer is the most common cause of belt failure. Belt costs range from $6.00 to $19.00. The service call and labor can easily add $40.00 to $60.00.

Part #2: The Dryer Heating Element

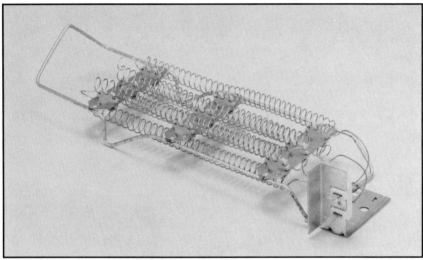

The element used on an electric dryer is 220 volts. Prices vary from $25.00 to $75.00. Service call and labor will add another $60.00 to $150.00.

Part #3 The Thermostat

The thermostat is used to shut off the heat when the air on the inside of the drum is the desired temperature. Each thermostat is set at a different temperature. A dryer may have four of them. Each costs between $15.00 and $45.00. Service and labor charges will normally be between $65.00 $150.00.

I'll tell you how to install most of the parts I listed here later in this chapter.

PART II: SETUP:

Here are some "do's and don'ts."

Do's:

Do make sure that your dryer is connected to a 220 volt power source and is perfectly level. The dryer will work with 110 volt power, but you are starving the equipment for energy and will end up burning up the dryer. Having your dryer working in an uneven condition will cause extra wear on rollers and felt pads and will cause expensive service problems.

Do make sure that the dryer is vented to the outside. Venting a gas dryer into the air can kill you and your family by infusing carbon monoxide and countless other poisons into the air. Venting an electric dryer into the inside may not kill you, but it will still inject impurities from chlorine bleach, fabric softener, lint and dust, etc., into the air and adversely effect your family's lungs and allergies. Over a period of time the chlorine will even corrode your plumbing.

Do make certain that the length of the vent line running between the dryer and the vent is not more than 14 feet with a metal elbow at the dryer and the vent.

Do make certain that the dryer vent line is the "old fashioned" rigid metal vent.

In chapter 5, I wrote about the defects of flexible plastic vent lines. I know flexible plastic vent lines are easier to install. But please folks, do not use them. They are illegal in some areas. They are nothing but fire traps and could kill you.

Don'ts:

Do not use screws to fasten the joints of the vent line together. Use duct tape for fastening. Screws form little lint traps inside the vent line and can cause a fire hazard.

Do not dry vegetable oil soaked dishcloths in your dryer after washing. They still contain enough oil to be a fire hazard and could burn your house down.

Do not store flammable materials near or on top of the dryer.

Do not close laundry room doors or restrict the amount of fresh air available to the dryer. You need 200 cubic feet of air per minute to operate the dryer properly.

Don't dry fluffy sweaters using fabric static sheets.

Don't operate your dryer while you shop, sleep, or are not in the vicinity. A dryer is a very handy, but potentially a very dangerous appliance. Please believe me, ten minutes of inattention could cost you your house, maybe your loved ones lives.

PART III: USE:

When you load a dryer put the clothes in singly, or at least in small handfuls. Do not just throw in a great big jumbled up lump of clothing into the dryer. It can throw the dryer out of kilter and cause permanent damage to the mechanism.

Never overload a dryer. The weight of the wet clothing can cause enough strain to break the rubber belts that turn the drum and will cause increased wear on the rollers causing premature replacement.

Under loading a dryer can also create problems because the clothing is not tumbling properly. If you only have a few things to dry add a couple of towels to the load and you will increase the dryer's efficiency.

Make certain that all clothing you dry in a dryer has gone through the spin dry cycle in the washing machine. If you notice that the clothing coming out of the washing machine after the spin dry cycle is still very wet it means that the washer was overloaded, or that the washer is not spinning fast enough for some reason.

Water draining from over wet clothing can drip on the ignitor or the electric heating element and cause a short. An accumulation of water inside the machine can cause rust inside the drum. Rust stains on your new white shirts can make you a very unhappy camper.

Always clean the lint filter after every use. Letting the filter get plugged up can cause a fire and will certainly impede the air flow, wasting energy dollars and increasing the wear on your clothing.

Older dryers have a very high heat factor and dry clothing more rapidly than modern dryers. The older models are not nearly as energy efficient and are much harder on your garments.

PART IV: MAINTENANCE:

Monthly:

Wash the lint screen out with mild soap and water. Just for the heck of it, take your lint screen over to the sink, hold it flat and pour a hand full of water over the mesh.

See how slowly it goes through the mesh? If it's really bad, the water may not be able to penetrate at all. This is caused by the build up of detergent and fabric softener on the mesh fibers.

If water can't get through, air can't get through. To work at maximum efficiency, the air going through the dryer must exit at a factory specified rate. Build up on the lint filter will slow down that rate and cause big service problems, in addition to increasing the fire hazard.

Every Year:

1. Once a year you need to give the inside of your dryer a complete cleaning. To do this you will have to pull the plug on the dryer and remove either the front or the rear panel of the dryer. Then take a refrigerator brush and the vacuum cleaner tool hose and suck up all the lint that has accumulated around the inside of the machine. You will be amazed at how much lint there is.

Take special care to clean around the ends of the motor. Making these areas lint free is vital to the longevity of the dryer motor. When air cannot go through the motor, the motor will overheat and cause premature failure.

You are going to have to get down on the floor to do this job properly. Get a flashlight and shine the light into all the nooks and crannies of the drier. Where-ever there is a hint of lint dust, get rid of it.

The screams that you hear are from the service industry. If you and the other appliance owners would just follow this one piece of advice and clean all the dust out of your machines, you would cost the service industry hundreds of millions of dollars in service charges.

2. Exterior dryer vent flaps often wedge open. This can cause trouble three ways: #1 It allows heat to escape from your house during the winter. #2 It makes your dryer extra cold during the winter and adds to drying time. #3 It allows little critters to climb into the vent line. I have actually had to remove birds nests complete with little birds from dryer vents.

Once a year, go to the outside of your house and check to see that the dryer vent is moving smoothly. Clean it thoroughly. Make sure that the vent flap hinges are moving freely.

3. Take the vent line off and give it a thorough cleaning. You want to get all the lint that has attached itself to the inner surface of the vent out of the vent line. Take the rigid vent line outside, take the elbows off either end. Run your garden hose through the vent line. Clean it out thoroughly.

PART V: TROUBLE SHOOTING

Dryer problems always get worse. When you notice a problem, fix it right away. Procrastination will only cause more damage and a much bigger bill.

Most dryers tops will pop up. Sometimes a few screws have to be removed. Once the top is up, only the removal of a few screws are needed to take the front panel off. Each make has something different to do for easy access. Your best bet is to call a service company and ask them to tell you how to do it over the phone. You can do most simple repairs yourself with just a little advice.

Major manufacturers publish a repair manual for each product in their line. The best time to buy it is when you get the machine.

OK, you probably have a two year warranty and don't care what happens for the next two years. Good, wait two years, then stop by your parts store and buy the manual.

Dryer repair should not intimidate you. Just quit procrastinating and buy the manual and we will fix most of the problems together.

PROBLEM: The dryer is on the bum, how do I open this thing up and see what's wrong?

It's very simple if you bought your service manual. If you didn't, try the instructions I just gave you.

PROBLEM: The dryer is starting to squeak.

A dryer that starts to squeal or squeak has to be serviced immediately. If you don't fix it immediately, the problem will get worse rapidly.

The squealing has probably been caused by an over heating motor, caused by lint build up. The permanently oiled bearings have run dry and there are no oil caps.

The common solution is to replace the motor. This doesn't work every time, but I have saved thousands of motors over the years by going to the store and getting a can of turbine oil and lubricating the shaft.

If you want to try and save your electric motor, try this. Take the motor out of the dryer. Place it on its end. Drop 20 to 30 drops of turbine oil down the shaft. Again, I emphasize turbine oil. Other kinds of an oil may turn into the consistency of caramel and make the problem even worse.

After the turbine oil has soaked down the shaft, turn the motor over and drop 20 to 30 more drops of turbine oil down the opposite shaft. Replace the motor, cross your fingers and see if the motor is back running in quiet condition. If it has, you have saved yourself the price of an electric motor. Keep oiling it annually.

If the motor still squeals, replace the motor.

PROBLEM: The dryer is working OK, but there is a rumbling noise.

Good thing you decided to check this out. The most common reason for a rumbling noise, is that one or both of the drum rollers have worn down and need to be replaced.

Take the drum out of the dryer and inspect the rollers that support the revolving drum. If either of them shows wear, replace both of them. The reason that you replace both is that if you just replace one roller, the newer roller will be slightly larger than the older roller and will throw the dryer out of kilter repeating the problem.

When you do this, it is a good idea to carefully inspect the drum felt seals at the front and back of the dryer. While the drum was rotating out of kilter, it was wearing down the felt seals. When the felt seals are worn, air is not moving in the specified pattern and it takes longer to dry each load. More important, the gap which appears between the felt seal and the rotating drum may allow a small piece of fabric to fall through the edge of the tub into the burner chamber and start a fire.

PROBLEM: The dryer drum has stopped rotating.

Probable cause is a broken dryer belt. These are amazingly simple to replace. Just make sure you get the right size belt from the service department. Every make situates the belt housing slightly differently, so if you take the front panel off the dryer and see that the belt is broken, be sure to consult your service manual. Before you get the replacement belt, check out the idler pulley. That is the small spring mounted wheel that keeps the tension on the dryer belt.

The idler pulley has an amazing amount of wear and has a relatively high failure rate. Make sure that it is rotating freely and not squealing. If it is squealing, replace it at the same time you replace the belt. If you don't, you will probably have to replace it six months from now.

By the way, to effect this repair, you have to take the drum out of the dryer. This provides an excellent opportunity to clean the dryer thoroughly. Please take the opportunity and make the inside of the dryer look like new when it is reassembled.

PROBLEM: The little pulley that keeps pressure on the dryer belt is squealing.

We talked about the idler pulley in the last tip. It receives so much wear that it can fail while the belts are still in good condition. If it is squealing, it should be replaced. It's easy to do, but each make is a little bit different, so consult your service manual.

PROBLEM: The dryer tumbles OK, but there is no heat.

Electric Dryers:

Failure of electric elements on dryers are quite often caused by the consumer either not having the proper kind of venting, or not supplying the dryer with sufficient power. Both are equally deadly to the dryer.

First thing, check the circuit box to see if you're lucky. If the 220 circuit breaker key has popped, push it in again and see if the dryer operates.

If your home has an old fuse box, you may have two 110 volt fuses supplying the 220 volts needed to run the dryer. If one of them blows and the dryer is still getting 110 volts of electricity, the motor will still work and rotate the drum, but the heating element will be starved.

If you are lucky, all you have to replace is the fuse. You wouldn't believe how hostile homeowners get when they have to pay for a $ 50 service call and all the guy does is replace a fuse. If you are unlucky, the heating element has been trying to operate on an energy starved basis and the heating element has burned out.

When the heating element has burned out for any reason, it needs to be replaced. You can do it yourself if you follow the service manual instructions carefully. Be sure to pull the plug on your dryer before you take the panels off the dryer. Consult your service manual for proper element specifications.

Gas Dryers:

The gas valve has to be checked out by experts. But that doesn't mean you have to pay for a service call. The gas valve assembly is easily removed by the consumer, and you will be amazed at how much money you can save by doing the leg work yourself.

On gas dryers there is usually a panel or front door which comes off to give you access to the gas valve assembly. You will find a shut off valve right at the end of the internal gas line. Shut off the gas by turning the shut off valve one half turn .

Disconnect the brass coupling nut at the beginning of the valve assembly. Pull the electrical connections and remove the screws which hold the valve assembly in place. Each dryer model is designed so that the gas valve assembly is positioned differently.

Once you have disconnected the gas valve assembly take it in to a parts and service company and have it checked out on the work bench. The cost for this service is usually quite low. The service technician will tell you exactly what is wrong with the assembly and what needs to be done to correct it. Usually replacement parts are available right on the spot

While working around the ignitor, keep in mind that it is very delicate and will break with minimum pressure. Treat it gently.

Some of the newer gas dryers do not have an access plate in front. This means that you will have to remove the entire front panel to get at the valve assembly. You can do it, but be sure you get a service manual.

Also, no heroics. No smoking. Disconnect the electric plug before you start working with gas. Be careful to be involved only up to the level of your confidence.

Now, let's go back up to the kitchen. I don't know about you, but writing this book has really worked up my thirst. I think Valorie may have a couple of Canadian cold ones waiting for us.

APPENDIX

Manufacturers of Sear's Kenmore Appliances

Sears Major Appliances are made by Whirlpool, General Electric and/or White/Westinghouse.

Whirlpool makes Refrigerators, Gas Ranges, Dishwashers, Washers and Dryers.

GE makes Refrigerators, Electric Ranges and Dishwashers.

White/Westinghouse makes the Kenmore Stacked Washer.

Corporate Ownership

AB Electrolux, a Sweedish Company, owns
White/Westinghouse which makes the following brand names:
**White/Westinghouse, Coronado, Frigidaire, Gibson,
Kelvinator, Sears' Kenmore Stacked Washer.**

General Electric makes *General Electric, Hot Point and RCA.*

Masco owns *Thermador/Waste King.*

Maytag owns *Gaffers and Stattler, and Jenn-Air and Norge*
which makes *Norge, Admiral, Crosley, Magic Chef and
some Montgomery Wards.*

Raytheon owns *Speed Queen, Amana, Caloric, Glenwood,
Modern Maid and Sunray.*

Tappan makes *Tappan and some Montgomery Wards*

Whirlpool owns *Whirlpool and Kitchen Aid.*

Manufacturers' Phone Numbers

Amana 800-843-0304
Athens 800-233-0498

Brown Stove Works 800-251-7224

Caloric/Modern Maid 800-843-0304
Carrier .... 800- CARRIER

Dacor 800-772-7748

Emmerson Quiet Kool 800-332-6658
Estate 800-253-1301

Fedders 800-332-6658
Frigidaire 800-451-7007

Gagneau 617-255-1766
General Electric and Hot Point 800-626-2000
Gibson 800-458-1445
Glenwood 800-759-1616

Insinkerator 800-558-5712

Jenn Air 800-688-1100

Kelvinator 800-323-7773
Kitchen-Aid 800-422-1230

Maycor 800-688-1120
Maytag 800-688-9900
Meile 800-843-7231

O'Keefe & Merritt 800-537-5530

Peerless Premier 800-858-5844

Roper 800-447-6737

Sanyo 800-421-5013
Sharp 800-447-4700
Speed Queen 800-843-0304
Sub Zero 800-222-7820

Tappan 800-537-5530
Thermador 800-735-4328

Welbilt 516-365-5040
White/Westinghouse 800-245-0600
Whirlpool 800-253-1301

Index

Biographical Notes

Joseph Ernest Roger Gagnon was born on December 3, 1941, in Timmins, Ontario, Canada, where his father was Chief of Police. He is a veteran of the Canadian Armed Forces, a former hockey player who still plays about five games a week, and a permanent resident of the United States since 1961.

Joe began his career in the major home appliance industry 30 years ago. Starting as a service technician for one of the major manufacturers, he worked his way up to regional service manager, instructor, customer relations manager and sales manager, before buying his own retail store, Carmack Appliance, in Garden City, Michigan. He is an active member and past president of the Garden City Chamber of Commerce

Outraged by some of the deceptive practices he found in the field, Joe became a volunteer investigator and expert witness for Esther Shapiro's Department of Consumer Affairs in Detroit. He also acted as a consultant to the office of the Attorney General of the State of Michigan and spearheaded drives, in conjunction with several Michigan state legislators, to upgrade Michigan's consumer protection laws and outlaw the use of slinky plastic or vinyl covered vent lines on clothes dryers.

Gagnon is president elect of the Great Lakes Chapter of S.O.C.A.P., The Society of Consumer Affairs Professionals in Business., a nation-wide organization of corporate consumer affairs executives, working to promote the consumer interest.

He has had his own listener call in radio show since 1985, his own cable TV show since 1989, and writes a newspaper column and do other projects like this book in his spare time.

**Ask your retailer about more
Master Handyman books.**

$14.95

"A treasure trove of answers to the most asked 'How To' questions...the book tells the easiest way to do many of the hardest cleaning and fix-up chores."
Kathleen Kavaney Zuleger
Book Review

$2.95

"Takes all the confusion out of deck care! Gives simple, easy to follow directions on how to keep your deck looking great. *Glenn Haege's COMPLETE DECK CARE GUIDE cuts through all the advertising claims. It is the Do-It-Yourselfer's only complete, unnbiased source of answers.*"

$14.97

$12.95

"Finally: a guide to interior do-it-yourself painting which follows a very simple yet information packed step-by-step format!...A very basic, essential home reference"
The Bookwatch

"Haege makes it easy for anyone smart enough to lift a paint can lid... to solve a particular painting problem."
The Detroit News

"Writing for paint retailers, contractors, and homeowners alike, Haege vends plenty of practical information organized into step-by-step procedures for everything..."
George Hampton
Booklist
American Library Association

TO: Master Handyman Press, Inc.
P.O. Box 1498
Royal Oak, MI. 48068-1498

Please send me copies of the following books:
All books are sold with a 100% money back, satisfaction guaranty:

___ FIX IT FAST & EASY! @ $14.95 each = $ _____
___ TAKE THE PAIN OUT OF PAINTING!
  - INTERIORS - @ $14.97 each = $ _____
___ TAKE THE PAIN OUT OF PAINTING!
  -EXTERIORS- @ $12.95 each = $ _____
___ Glenn Haege's COMPLETE DECK
  CARE GUIDE @ $ 2.95 each = $ _____
___ FIRST AID from the Appliance Doctor,
  Joe Gagnon @ $14.97 each = $ _____

Total $ _____

Michigan Residents: Please add 4% Sales Tax.

Shipping: $2 for the first book and $1 for each additional. If ordering only Glenn Haege's COMPLETE DECK CARE GUIDE, pay a shipping charge of $1 only.
   SHIPPING: _____

Total $ _____

Name: _____
Phone No _____
Address: _____
_____ ZIP: _____

Credit Card Information. Please fill out if you wish to charge.
Please charge my _____ Visa _____ Master Card
Expiration Date: _____ Card # _____
Name on Card: _____
Signature: _____

Mail to:

Master Handyman Press, Inc.
P.O. Box 1498
Royal Oak, MI 48068-1498